On a Variety of Subjects

On a Variety of Subjects
Paul M. Angle

With an Introduction by
Hoke Norris

Chicago Historical Society

The Caxton Club, Chicago

Publication of this book was made possible
in part by the PHILIP K. WRIGLEY FUND
of the Chicago Historical Society

Library of Congress Catalog Card Number: 74-82578
ISBN Number: 0-913820-04-0

Printed by Edwards Brothers, Ann Arbor
Designed by Cameron Poulter

Contents

Introduction

This book is published by two organizations concerned with history, and they dedicate it to the life and works of the historian Paul M. Angle. It consists of his own selections from among his many works—selections which demonstrate the breadth and depth of his scholarship. After he made his choice it became my pleasure and honor to write this Introduction. In preparation I interviewed Paul in the Eighteenth-Century Dining Room at the Chicago Historical Society, of which he was director for twenty years and secretary and editor for five more. The choice of place was fortunate—it helped put us in mind of the past which has been Paul's concern for more than half a century (as did Lincoln Park, the Lincoln Monument that lay beyond the east windows, and the Angles' venerable frame house on Lincoln Park West, a few blocks from the Society, where I later talked to him further). The past lay visible all about us.

I took on this job with the hope that perhaps I could make some atonement for a neglect that Paul had good-naturedly reproved me for a few years before. I had made a talk on Illinois writers—by writers meaning, in the narrow definition, the authors of fiction, plays, and poetry, which are my specialty—and Paul made the point later that historians were too often neglected in discussions of a region's or nation's artistic heritage. I agreed then, and do now. The good historian is also the good writer—he is an artist—and I am glad to offer the selections that follow as incontrovertible evidence of that truth.

Since this is Paul Angle's book, I shall to the extent possible introduce it in his own words. What we lose (if anything) in discursiveness we will compensate for by a good measure of Paul's style and idiom.

I asked Paul how the book came into being. Referring to Clement M. Silvestro, the recent director of the Chicago Historical Society, Paul told me:

"Silvestro said to me some years ago now, 'I don't want to back the hearse up to the door of your house, but I would like to look forward to a time when the Society could issue a collection of your writing, perhaps posthumously, if you have no objection.' And I said I'd be pleased to have that happen. So he communicated with Roger Shugg, the former director of the University of Chicago Press, and Shugg said, 'Posthumous hell! Why wait till the guy dies? Go ahead and do it now.' At the same time the Caxton Club, which issues a publication now and then and of which I've been a member for a good many years, became interested in something of the same kind. And so they decided upon joint publication and left it to me to make the selections. Well, I made the selections I did because I have always been typed as a writer about Abraham Lincoln and the Civil War. I thought that some of perhaps my best writing was outside of those fields, and much of it was in places where very few people would see it, like an address at the William L. Clements Library, in Ann Arbor, that appeared in the *Michigan Alumnus,* and how many people outside of University of Michigan alumni would see it? And yet I like it and thought it was good. [It appears here as "Across the Board: Reflections on Book Collecting."] Others appeared in fugitive places, or at least places where they would be seen by very few people, and there was one piece which I've included which has never been published at all. It was a piece I called 'In the Service of Clio.' I didn't want to publish that for a number of years, because too many people were mentioned, not always in a favorable light, and could readily have been identified. And I somehow wasn't for hurting anybody's feelings. But now anybody that would be offended by it is long since gone. So this was my motivation in making the selection I did—that, and the fact that I liked the pieces. I wanted to demonstrate that I've got a broader range than Lincoln and the Civil War."

And just so did a book come into being. The range Paul demonstrates is broader, much broader—not only Lincoln and the Civil War, but also the Pilgrims, Parson Weems, Horatio Alger, Jr., Emily Post, John Brown's Body, reminiscences of life in Ohio and in Chicago, the agricultural and industrial development of the Middle West, a short story, strike wars, a hanging, and a memoir about a friend.

And now, a brief look backward.

Paul McClelland Angle was born in Mansfield, Ohio, on Christmas Day in 1900. His father was a grocer. Of the young Paul Angle's life in that Ohio town during the century's young years, of his parents and of his own growing up, you may read with pleasure in "Recollections I" and "Recollections II" ("Recollections III" is a delightful bit of gone but beautifully remembered Chicago). He attended Oberlin College in 1918–19 and then transferred to the more hospitable and helpful campus of Miami University. ("And for God's sake," he said, the historian in him rising in indignation, "don't say Miami of Ohio. Florida, where that upstart school is located, was still a province of Spain when Miami University was founded.")

Although both in high school and college—"for eight long years"—Paul played football, he was nevertheless valedictorian of his high-school graduating class, and at Miami University made Phi Beta Kappa in three years and graduated *magna cum laude*.

On the Miami campus was a co-ed named Vesta Verne Magee. How can one write about Paul without writing also about Vesta? I asked him to tell me about her.

"She was one class behind me. I was in the class of 1922, she was in '23. I came from north-central Ohio and she came from southwestern Ohio, a little town called Piqua. Eventually we became engaged, and we got married three or four years later. She was pretty—still is, as a matter of fact—and intelligent, and had a lot of personality. That's about it. Who knows about these things?"

He continued:

"The first intimation that I might have some skill with words came from an English instructor when I was a freshman at Oberlin College. That's about the only thing I got out of the place. After class one day he told me that he would like to have me stop at his house for a few minutes. That I did, of course. The ungracious idiot never invited me beyond the front hall, but he did say something like 'That last theme you turned in was one of the best pieces of writing I've seen in years. In style it was lean but your imagery was vivid. I hope you will keep it up. Goodbye.'

"Well, after graduating from Miami, I had a fling at the insurance business which demonstrated to me that whatever I might be suited for, life insurance was not it. With the intention of going into college teaching I wangled a scholarship at the University of Illinois, and emerged with a master's degree. Scholastically, it was a wasted year, but it did give me the opportunity to read a lot of books which I had heard about but never got around to. That year left me in debt, so I got a job with the American Book Company selling school textbooks.

"After twelve months I had paid off my obligations and was ready to take off. The president of Miami offered me an assistant professorship and I was about to take it when an opportunity opened up in Springfield, Illinois. There some public-spirited citizens had revived an organization called the Lincoln Centennial Association with the intention of turning it into a small historical society that would conduct research into the life of Lincoln. On the recommendation of a professor at Illinois I was asked to come to Springfield to be interviewed for the job of secretary. I knew nothing about Abraham Lincoln, but I did manage to read most of Lord Charnwood's biography on the train from eastern Ohio to Springfield. The job there paid $3,000 a year instead of the $2,000 I would have received at Miami. And besides, this was 1925, when you could quit one job on Saturday and get another Monday morning.

"The Lincoln Centennial Association, later called the Abraham Lincoln Association, and I got along. I had various responsibilities, one of them being to turn out a four-page *Bulletin* every three months. When I showed the copy for the first one to Logan Hay, the Association's president, he asked me to take it to George W. Bunn, Jr., a young businessman who, after college, had been a reader for the old Doran publishing firm. Bunn looked it over and commented: 'This is good. Your prose is lean, logical, almost French. Yet you have some color too. Keep writing.' I took his advice to heart."

The career thus launched eventually brought Paul to Chicago and the directorship of the Chicago Historical Society, and through the writing, collaborating on, or editing of eighteen books (this is the nineteenth), the supervision of the Society's program and collections, the preparation and execution of its enlargement and its publications, and the presiding over of its growth in influence and significance as a member of the scholarly community and as a popular institution in Chicago. Along the way he picked up some skills and knowledge not overtly associated with his jobs in Springfield and in Chicago. He learned to wheel and deal politically when necessary for appropriations or for getting rid of political jobholders; when not to close the door of his office; how to hang pictures; how to deal with crooks and with scholars, and more.

In Springfield, to go back, he became taken up with the Lincoln story. "I wrote a piece exposing the Ann Rutledge myth which Albert J. Beveridge, whom I had come to know, tried to get published for me, but without success. Nevertheless when I published it in the Association's *Bulletin,* it did attract some attention."

Paul was ready when, in the pages of the venerable *Atlantic Monthly,* he spotted the first installment of a three-part series entitled "Lincoln the Lover," by Wilma Frances Minor. It purported to be based on letters and diaries supporting the existence of a romance between Abraham Lincoln and Ann Rutledge. The process of detection, and its consequence, you can read about in "The Minor Lincoln Collection: A Criticism," the first article in this book. It is as fascinating as a detective story—it is in fact a story of detection, of the discovery of ambiguities, contradictions, historical impossibilities, errors of fact and of style. Paul did the job so well that the editor of the *Atlantic* himself published the exposé. I asked Paul what became of Wilma Frances Minor.

"I don't know," he replied. "She was a newspaperwoman, and her mother was a spiritualist medium. She confessed finally that she got all the stuff from her mother, who claimed she was in communication with Lincoln. Lincoln had enjoined her to write it down, and had elaborated the situations and so forth—such was the claim. Miss Minor believed in her mother's spiritualistic powers, but one of her deceptions was that instead of presenting the material as *that,* as material written down during seances, she pretended that it consisted of actual diaries and letters. And that's all been in limbo—that is, the story about the spiritualist mother—until the spring of 1974. That's because Edward Weeks, who later became editor of the *Atlantic,* and was on the staff of the magazine when this whole thing took place, has just published his autobiography, *My Green Age: A Memoir,* in which he tells, for the first time, as much as the *Atlantic* ever found out, and as much as we are ever likely to know, about the episode." Altogether, the hoax can be compared only with Clifford Irving's claim to have interviewed Howard Hughes, that came along many years later.

With Paul's literary-historical career thus launched, "Requests for book reviews came in, and I began to think of books that might add something to the existing knowledge of Abraham Lincoln. I mined that vein for the next twenty years, when I came to the conclusion that I had said everything about Lincoln that I wanted to say, and then I turned to other subjects. I have done a couple of Lincoln books since then, but by force of circumstance rather than from desire. In fact I've never had any compulsive desire to write simply for the sake of putting words on paper. I have written for two reasons. First, because I had something to say, or thought I had something to say. My second reason, quite frankly, was to make money. I've been able to support my family in a manner that would have been impossible if I hadn't written." The Angles have two children, Paula and John Edwin.

"There's another thing a little unusual about my writing habits too. I have four dictionaries, but the one I use almost exclusively is Webster's *Secondary School Dictionary,* copyrighted in 1925. Of course, for scientific words that have become part of the language in the last forty-five years, I have to resort to later works of reference, but I hold that if a word isn't in that high-school dictionary I'd better not use it. And I don't. As for my writing method—I have never been able to think at a typewriter. So I write with a soft pencil on a yellow pad, which gives me an opportunity to revise as I go along. Then, with two fingers, I transcribe what I have written on a twenty-year-old Smith Corona portable. That gives me a chance to revise, because there seems to be a different rhythm in typing, even slow as I am, from that of writing by hand. I've deviated from this method only once, when I dictated a book to a very efficient stenographer. Although the result was successful, and I was pleased with it, I have since reverted to my primordial method because I'm happier with it."

These are the statements of a "pro"—the honest admissions of one who writes for a living. I was also impressed by Paul's statement that after twenty years he had said all he wanted to say about Lincoln. Some writers never know when to leave a subject. And some never learn that it is often true that a few words are better than many. Paul says of "The Lincoln Funeral," in this volume, that his first draft ran to thirty pages. Its final version is barely two. There stands the wastebasket, filled with rejected pages. The writer's best friend is his wastebasket.

"I think that in the last analysis the writer, any writer," Paul said, "has to be his own severest critic. He has to be able to divorce himself from the fact of authorship, if he possibly can, and look at what he has written with as nearly an impartial eye as he can achieve. And he has to be able to say to himself, 'Well, it doesn't matter if I spent two hours writing this page, it's no damn good. I've got to throw it away and start again.' I know that on one little piece of the kind that I've used in here, these evaluations of older and influential books, I tried nine times to get it within the limits imposed, about 310 words, and in a form that satisfied me. I had the wastebasket half-filled with discarded sheets. I thought after I had thrown that batch away I really should have saved them. It would have been an interesting example of how a writer discards, time after time, before he achieves a form which finally satisfies him. Now that isn't always the case, of course. Sometimes you can do it right off the bat and get it in reasonably satisfactory shape. A girl in our neighborhood asked me to do a piece for the Old Town Triangle program book for the art fair last year. She wanted about 600 words on Old Town as I have seen it change and develop in twenty-five years. Well, I got to thinking about that around 10:30 one night, and I pulled up a pad and wrote the whole darn thing by midnight. I don't think I changed a word. It came out right, right from the beginning. All too often, that doesn't happen. And there's one thing I thoroughly believe in, if time is available: write something and then let it simmer for a couple of weeks. Then go back to it. You return to it with a fresh point of view. I do that repeatedly."

I asked Paul why one should write and study history—what were its rewards. I had been impressed by "A Shelf of Lincoln Books," which contains a description of what, with his knowledge of history, he could see as he looked out from his house in Springfield across a stretch of land that once had been the Sangamon County fairgrounds. He could see the Republicans there on an August day in 1860, and Lincoln, and the Illinois farm boys drilling for civil war—altogether a splendid evocation of the past.

"I think that a knowledge of history enriches one's life," Paul responded to my question. "It lends another dimension to living. I think also that history is in a sense a guide to the present and future. The example that comes to mind right now is that of Harry Truman. During the Second World War he was head of the committee on the conduct of the war. Now Truman was an avid reader of history, and one of the first things he did to prepare himself for that job was to read the full reports of the Civil War committee on the conduct of that war, and then resolve that he was not going to do anything like that with the committee that was under his jurisdiction. And he didn't. And the committee on the conduct of the war, the Truman Committee as it was called, was an extremely valuable adjunct of government, primarily because the man at the head of it knew the history of an earlier committee, eighty years before. Let's come right down to the present. If Nixon had known anything about history, there wouldn't have been this attempt to cover up the Watergate deal. He should have known about Grover Cleveland for instance. When he was running for the presidency it was discovered that he had an illegitimate child. They brought this to the candidate's attention and said, 'How're we going to handle it?' 'Well,' he said, 'tell 'em the truth. Sure, I had an illegitimate child. I've taken care of it, and taken care of the mother for the last thirty years. Let them make out of it what they want.' And I won't say the whole thing disappeared, but it didn't hurt him a darn bit. If he'd tried to cover that up, what would have happened? And of course you have the example, more recently, of the Harding scandals. Harding died, and Coolidge discovered how serious the whole Teapot Dome thing was, and promptly appointed special prosecution to get at the truth."

History also helps, does it not, to establish perspectives? I had in mind Paul's article about the celebration of the centennial of the Civil War—"Tragic Years: The Civil War and its Commemoration." Paul, I felt, knew when the hucksters took over, and knew the proper response when that observance got out of hand.

"About that time," he replied, "about 1960 or thereabouts, the *South Atlantic Quarterly* announced that it was going to ignore the Civil War centennial unless somebody came up with an article so unusual and so distinctive that they had to print it. Well, I took that kind of as a challenge, so I sat down and wrote this piece and sent it to them and they took it right away."

I was able to inform him that a couple of Southerners, Ralph McGill and Paul Green, agreed with him about the celebration—that McGill wrote of "increasing numbers of persons wandering about the South wearing sleezy imitations of Confederate uniforms, growing beards, renewing old hatreds, making ancient wounds bleed again, reviving Ku Klux Klans"; and that the poet and playwright Green, in a passage about the reenactment of the Battle of Manassas,. recorded that "at least one general fell off his horse (General Stonewall Jackson it was, from Lenox, Massachusetts), and other officers and enlisted men went wandering and astray in the woods . . . 'died' in the wrong place . . . unseen, unwept, unhonored, unsung, but not unstung."

Such antics, Paul said, dishonored both the past and the present. I suggested that the best way to honor the past was to write about it well, and cited a passage of his that had struck me for its force, brevity and beauty—the opening paragraph of "Historical Miniatures." The reader will come to it later, but I'll quote it here anyway.

> The tide was right, the wind fair. The departure of the ship the English Pilgrims hoped would take them to a permanent haven in the New World could not be delayed. For eleven years, unwelcome in their own land, they had lived among the friendly Dutch of Leiden. Now they were sailing from the nearby port of Delshaven. Not all could go, so those who were to remain gathered on the deck to say farewell. Kneeling, their cheeks wet with tears, the Englishmen heard their pastor ask God's blessing. As they embraced each other, many for the last time, the stolid Hollanders who looked on in curiosity found their own eyes dim. But, in the words of William Bradford, one of their leaders,"they knew they were pilgrimes, and looked not much on those things, but lift up their eyes to the heavens, their dearest countrie, and quieted their spirits."

I asked Paul how he managed to recreate that scene so vividly.

"Well," he replied, "that I suppose is partly imagination. And yet most of those statements are based on fact. Take 'The tide was right, the wind fair'—they'd been trying to get away for a week or two, and it was only on this particular day that this combination of natural circumstances permitted them to. And, well, you use Bradford's journal. I think I relied pretty heavily upon the account in Channing's multi-volume history of the United States. I don't recall what else

I used there, but that passage is carefully based on fact insofar as I could ascertain it.

"As I say somewhere, my approach to history is similar to that of my favorite historian, Francis Parkman—'to recreate the past for the benefit of the present.' If I have made a part of the past come to life, then I'm satisfied. Now in my opinion the ability to do that depends on several qualities. In the first place, you have to be accurate. That I think should be the guiding principle in writing all history. I would never, for example, manufacture conversation. You view even conversations that have been written out with skepticism, knowing how hard it is to remember the exact words that anyone has used. I also think that one must write simply, and with clarity. Then I think an historian, if he's to do his job, must bring out the essential drama of any situation, if drama is there. It isn't always. There are certain things that you have to deal with in history that are not dramatic at all; some of them are dull. But if there is drama, the historian should try to recreate it. My aim is always to make a particular segment of the past come to life, so that the present may view it as it happened. Above all, it must be readable. One of the best examples I can cite is my old friend, now unfortunately long since dead, Lloyd Lewis, who never wrote a page that wasn't readable, and yet never distorted the truth to achieve readability. You don't have to choose between scholarship and readability. I can cite historical writing that is highly readable but isn't worth the paper it's written on, because the writer went to the other extreme. He sacrificed fidelity for readability. But read-ability—that certainly is *one* of the aims. This point of view is of course hopelessly old-fashioned.

"History I think has fallen on evil ways, in the colleges and universities. These people have become enamored of computers, statistical methods, the combination of disciplines in the writing of a book, and they've gotten away from one of the primary appeals of history, which is to tell a story. And I am convinced that the dominance they have achieved in the universities is the primary reason why students are shunning history in droves.

"Tell the truth, tell what happened in the past, and don't get into statistical explanations and all this kind of thing. Forget about what sociology or psychology can bring to the explanation of a given period. Write it as a historian, as a sensible person. I think that this emphasis upon all of these new tools, and very narrow subjects, is all wrong. You can discover what they're up to if you take the time to read the *Journal of American History,* and you can't imagine yourself wanting to read one out of fifty books that are reviewed there. Frankly, I don't see how most of the product of the present-day historian gets into print. I don't know who wants to read it. Their works are somewhat less interesting and not nearly as important as the *World Almanac.* I never taught a minute in my life and never regretted the lack, and some of these academic historians don't think you're a *professional* historian unless you do teach in a university and have the union card—the Ph.D." In a couple of his pieces herein, Paul refers to the useless meetings academic historians think they must attend, and to their places of employment as "the graves of Academe."

"Of course they're not all like that. Allan Nevins and Bruce Catton are among the best of the moderns. Dan Boorstin writes sound books that are also interesting and readable. So do others. And so do some whom the so-called professionals would scorn. Barbara Tuchman is one. And even the poets and novelists have done creditable work: Archibald MacLeish, for instance, in *Conquistador,* and Stephen Vincent Benet in *John Brown's Body,* which I think is one of the greatest books of the twentieth century. As my old friend Benjamin Platt Thomas said, 'history is meaningless unless it's readable.' " Paul writes about Thomas in "To the Memory of a Friend."

My next question concerned the times in which the modern historian had to work. Paul Angle was born three years before the Wright brothers made their flight at Kitty Hawk. In his lifetime, then, all that we associate with flying has come into being—speed of travel, monumentally fatal plane crashes, aerial warfare and bombing, the shift from piston to jet—and also most of the other developments that we associate with our day: the general acceptance and expansion of the theories of Darwin, Freud, and Einstein; atomic energy, atomic medicine, atomic warfare; radio, television; space travel; the crushing consequences of the automobile; the extinction of animals and birds, the pollution of air and water, and measures taken to resist that pollution; the proliferation of computers and their applications. The whole seemed enough to overwhelm any historian.

Paul accepted the question with a historian's tranquility. "I think it's all had a very strong effect upon the generalists," he said. "Take a person like J. C. Furnas. His *The Americans: A Social History of the United States 1587–1914* is a great book. He has to deal with those things you've mentioned— some of them anyway. That may be the reason he quit at 1914—the subject was getting too complex. Now, to change the reference a little bit, the proliferation of records alone is staggering. Of course we don't have records of many of the great changes that have taken place in the last fifty or sixty years because the telephone has supplanted the written memorandum and the letter as a source of information and communication. But even so, the proliferation of records, limited though they may be, has practically eliminated the possibility of a great deal of first-hand research. The records are too complex. You could spend a lifetime going through them, and get no more than a glimpse of history. So I think the method of the historian is going to have to change. You see criticisms of an author now and then because he has not used manuscript sources. He can't! He'd be spending a lifetime if he consulted the manuscripts. One example of that, and criticism made of it, is Bob Howard's recent book *Illinois: A History of the Prairie State,* which I think is a very good book. Some reviewer criticized Howard for not consulting manuscript sources. Well, my God, if he had tried to do that he'd have spent another ten years at work, and I'm not sure that it would have paid him. Just take the Horner manuscripts alone, or the Stevenson manuscripts— they just don't yield enough for the generalist to make consulting them thoroughly worthwhile. So I think there's going to have to be more and more reliance upon what the historian calls 'secondary sources,' rather than this interminable search among manuscripts. You can do that for certain periods in the past, but you can't do it for the present."

I was interested in another aspect of history—what creates the events that make history? I asked Paul, which comes first, event or man? Was history made by events acting on men, or men acting on events?

"Ah," he said with a smile, "that's an old one, and a good one. I don't know, exactly. I think it can be either way, or a combination of both. You can say, for example, that the Civil War resulted from a combination of men and events or forces acting on each other, interacting. The forces were slavery and anti-slavery, but the Southern fire-eaters did a great deal to bring those forces to a crisis, much more than anybody on the other side, more so than the abolitionists, who didn't do much, really, to bring on the war. In the present, with Watergate, to refer to *that* again, I can't see it in any other way than as a result of the machinations of evil men. There was no general movement or popular program or force that brought on that disgraceful series of events. They were largely created, man-made events, in a sense a superficial phenomenon—an ill-advised and crooked attempt to obtain what foolish people considered to be political advantage. Even the president's pretty obvious attempts to make the presidency far superior to other branches of government—even that stems largely from the attitude and philosophy of one man.

"On the other hand, events sometimes make history. The United States was more or less forced into World War II—it had little choice in the matter. But our involvement in Vietnam can be attributed to two or three individuals. I don't think anybody wanted to go to war in Vietnam. There certainly was no popular movement that took us there, or made us bomb Cambodia."

For most of Paul Angle's professional life he had been examining America's schizophrenia. By that I mean: Paul Angle's first subject, Lincoln, was a man of contradictions. He was a man of peace who served a peaceful period as a soldier in the Black Hawk War, opposed President Polk's

Mexican War and so lost popularity at home and did not seek reelection to Congress, and yet commanded the troops in the bloody strife of the Civil War. The United States created both the world's greatest democracy and its most depraved system of slavery. It is capable of both great violence and great charity: it defeats a foe, then recreates it with moral and economic aid. The violence of the frontier lives on in our lives long after it has served its dubious purpose. We cling to our guns; some of us are capable of murder in the night, and then gracious offers of a ride to a wayfaring stranger in the light of day. The Civil War purged the nation of slavery, though not of all its evils, and the violence in us lingers on.

Paul's most explicit examination of violence is to be found in the book that he considers to be his best, *Bloody Williamson*, extracts from which appear in "Rough Stuff I" and "Rough Stuff II." I asked him why he thought it to be his best work.

"Well," he said, "I suppose that book came closer to achieving what I really set out to do than any other. That's my own opinion of it, and I suppose that's why it's my favorite. And I think it's my favorite because I devised a style that was new to me, which I'd never attempted before. And I believe I pulled it off. I would call it the staccato style. Short sentences, short paragraphs, keeping the story moving. I'm inclined to write more discursively than I did in the book, but I thought that the situation called for a different kind of literary approach."

Paul has a copy of *Bloody Williamson* that was given to him by the Aurora Public Library—a copy thoroughly and neatly annotated in red ink by a reader whose father or husband was a Klansman and who was incensed by the author's examination of the Klan in southern Illinois. "How does Paul Angle explain this dirty crook Galligan?" demands the aroused annotator at one point. "Galligan's word good? Phooey!!" A couple of pages further on, about another character, "An old hypocrit!" and "More Paul Angle lies! Paul Angle never saw Young! So, how does he know!" And so on. Paul looks at these angry comments, and laughs. The criticism is sincere, even if misguided. Perhaps the comments grew out of a belief that Paul Angle should not have investigated the story at all. In fact, he writes in his Foreword:

Some of my Williamson County friends will criticize me for writing this book. They are sensitive about their county's history, and doubtless the more so because they know their own innate decency and friendliness, and realize that odium was brought upon them either by a small minority, or by a majority acting abnormally for short periods. . . . Others of my southern Illinois friends—a majority, I believe—will agree with my contention that no segment of the American past is immune to investigation, and that the story of Bloody Williamson, so long the province of the sensationalist, needs a thoroughgoing recital more than most.

This thoroughgoing recital—this story of gang wars, of the Klan, of labor strife and massacre—should teach America something about itself, about its violence. One remembers the Socratic notion that the unexamined life is not worth living, and Santayana's dictum that a people that forgets its history is condemned to live it. Here is Paul Angle on America's murderous proclivities, in his foreword to *Bloody Williamson:*

We Americans—and now I apply the term to the people who have occupied the present United States since the first English settlements in North America—have never been slow to resort to violence, sometimes in passion, sometimes in the conviction that legal processes were either inadequate or too slow in their operations; sometimes simply because the law interfered with what we wanted to do. . . . Its forms are as diverse as the emotions of our people, and its power to break through conventional barriers, and to thrive on itself, has been demonstrated in every part of the country and at every period in our history.

And after nearly three hundred pages of the bloody vendetta, the massacre, the Klan crusade, the gang war, Paul writes a conclusion: all these murderous events "revealed the frailty of social restraints."

> Conscience, it was shown, is a monitor easily disregarded, for a man can come to kill another without losing a half-hour's sleep. Against greed and other strong emotions the law is a weak barrier. Adamant adherence to principles can breed its own troubles. . . . Who knows what mixture of motives impelled the participants in the Klan crusade? What part was played by the rigid moralist's envy of the pleasures of sin? By the Protestant's deep-seated fear of the Catholic? By the desire of the old "American" to put the newer citizen . . . in his place? And note the almost constant presence of official incompetence or official corruption. Lack of respect for law. Venal public servants. Union labor and "free enterprise." Black man and white man. Old-fashioned morality and lax standards of conduct. Protestant and Catholic. "American" and foreigner. Shibboleths, trite antitheses, even windy rhetorical phrases. . . . The same conflicts are to be found in many another community. If they persist until passion displaces reason there will be other Herrins.

I have quoted from *Bloody Williamson* at some length because for me at least it summarizes a civilized man's abhorrence for the uncivilized acts of which his fellow man is not only capable but which he can accomplish with a gusto that leaves one aghast. The violent ones may prevail in a limited time and in a limited space, but between them and the rest of us there stand such men as Paul Angle, who by recording violence may prevent its repetition. In the recording, to face the truth, they may prevent *us,* the supposed nonviolent, from following our brother Cain to the bloody solution.

Hoke Norris

The Minor Lincoln Collection: *A Criticism*

In the fall of 1928 the *Atlantic Monthly,* the most
prestigious magazine in the country, announced, with
fanfare not in harmony with its staid tradition, that in its
December issue it would publish the first of a three-part
serial documenting fully the romance between Abraham
Lincoln and Ann Rutledge. The documentation consisted
of newly discovered letters which passed between the two
principals, together with diary entries and letters of
contemporaries, all woven together by the owner of the
collection, Wilma Frances Minor. The documents had not
only passed all physical tests of authenticity, but had also
been vouched for by two eminent Lincoln authorities, the
Rev. William E. Barton of Oak Park, Illinois, and Ida M.
Tarbell of New York City. Furthermore, the *Atlantic*
announced that for the first time in its history it was using
illustrations, facsimiles of several of the documents on
which the story was based.

When I saw the *Atlantic's* first installment I knew that
the Lincoln letters were spurious. At once I wrote and
published a special *Bulletin* of the Lincoln Centennial
Association denouncing the Lincoln letters as forgeries,
and casting grave doubt upon the authenticity of the
supporting material. Newspapers all over the country
hopped with glee upon this demonstration that a magazine
of impeccable reputation might after all be not quite lily
white. But Ellery Sedgwick, the *Atlantic's* editor, persisted
in his belief that he was presenting a genuine contribution
to the Lincoln story, and published the second and third
installments as scheduled.

By this time I had been joined by stalwart associates, notably Oliver R. Barrett of Chicago, the owner of an outstanding collection of Lincoln manuscripts, and Worthington C. Ford, former head of the Manuscripts Division of the Library of Congress and then editor of the Massachusetts Historical Society. Ford felt personally affronted by what he considered the dishonesty of Sedgwick, his fellow-townsman. The three of us bombarded every new installment of the great Lincoln story with press releases, and the newspapers had a heyday at the expense of the *Atlantic Monthly.*

In the end Sedgwick capitulated and asked me to write the exposure of the Minor Lincoln Collection that appears here, although I am not sure that he was ever completely convinced that he had been duped. I had not thought of including this article in this compilation until the recent Clifford Irving–Howard Hughes fraud gave it new relevance.

Those of us who engage in historical research are likely to assume that everyone will know what tests to apply in order to establish the authenticity of a series of historical documents, and will possess the knowledge necessary for the successful application of those tests. The assumption is unwarranted, of course. Rarely will all possible criteria suggest themselves even to highly intelligent persons without historical training, and more rarely still will they possess the specialized knowledge without which the criteria are useless.

In view of this fact it will be worth while at least to itemize the tests which a collection, such as the alleged Lincoln documents published serially in the *Atlantic* for December 1928, January and February 1929, should pass before its genuineness can be accepted. First come the purely physical criteria: Is the paper of the proper age, and is the ink that of the period in which the documents are supposed to have been written? Next, the soundness of the collection's pedigree, so to speak: Has it come down through a line of well-authenticated, reputable owners? Then, if the documents

Reprinted from the *Atlantic Monthly,* April 1929, pp. 516–24 purport to be the work of a well-known character, comes the question of handwriting. Does it resemble that of letters and papers of undoubted genuineness? More intangible, but very important, is the question of general content. Are the sentiments expressed in any given document in harmony with the known views of the person who is supposed to have written it, or even with his general character as established beyond dispute? Finally, do specific incidents mentioned in the challenged documents check with demonstrable historical fact?

It is not often that all of these tests can be brought to bear against a body of material so effectively as in the case of the Minor collection. Almost every item revealed such serious flaws that belief in the genuineness of the entire group became untenable. Recognizing this, the editor of the *Atlantic* not only published a statement withdrawing former expressions of confidence in the collection, but asked me, as one of those active in attacking its claims to credence, to state the case against it. In undertaking this, I hope I shall be pardoned for appropriating to my own use the contributions of Mr. Worthington C. Ford, Mr. Oliver R. Barrett, Mr. Louis A. Warren, Mr. Logan Hay, and Captain James P. Murphy, without which the prompt exposé of the character of these documents would not have been possible.

As soon as the collection was presented for publication, the *Atlantic* submitted specimens of the paper to a distinguished chemist for analysis. The report described it as "pure linen with a trace of cotton." Since modern paper is largely made from wood pulp, the presumption was that the paper of these documents was of sufficient age.

However, that is not a fact of positive importance. The first concern of every forger is to secure old paper, and on the whole it is easily accomplished. In this case a suspicious resemblance to the flyleaves of old books suggests the source from which it was obtained. There is another disquieting feature of physical appearance. Several of the documents are written in green ink. Green ink usually has an aniline dye as a coloring agent, and aniline dyes were not in use prior to the second half of the nineteenth century. However, the color of the ink could do no more than arouse suspicion, since inks of all colors have long been used to some extent. When the line of descent of the Minor collection was critically examined serious weaknesses appeared. The story of its formation and transmission was related with considerable explicitness. For various plausible reasons Lincoln and Ann Rutledge gave each other's letters to a common friend, Matilda Cameron. Matilda added her own diary, and the collection passed to Sally Calhoun, described as the daughter of John Calhoun, Lincoln's friend and benefactor. Sally added memoranda of conversations with her father and letters from Lincoln, and gave the entire group of documents to two friends, Margaret Morrison and Elizabeth Hirth. In time these joint owners transferred it to Elizabeth's brother, Frederick Hirth. With the addition of a letter Hirth is supposed to have received from Lincoln it attained its final form, and descended through Hirth's widow and Miss Minor's own mother to the present owner.

Examination, however, fails to reveal satisfactory evidence that the first two reputed owners of the collection, Matilda Cameron and Sally Calhoun, ever actually existed. Matilda is described as one of the eleven daughters of John Cameron of New Salem, and Ann's cousin as well as bosom friend. But the page from the Cameron family Bible on which the names and birth dates of the children were inscribed, now in the possession of Mrs. Edna Orendorff Macpherson of the Illinois State Historical Library, fails to record a Matilda among them.

However, in the family record only the first names and middle initials are given, and for three of the girls the middle initial was M. Might not that have stood, in one case, for Matilda? Matilda's diary destroys the possibility. In the entry dated July 10, 1833, occurs this statement: "I will keep everthing in my box James giv me last crismas. my first bow wuz James and *now Sam* Anns wuz first John an now Abe. she wuz 17 when she met John and I wuz 19 when I first met James." Since James and Matilda were lovers "last crismas," their first meeting could not have occurred later than 1832. If Matilda was then nineteen, she must have been born not later than 1813. But Vicana M., the second of the Cameron girls and the first to bear the middle initial M., was born on December 31, 1815. A daughter was born in 1813, but her name was Elizabeth P.

Equally conclusive is the argument against the existence of Sally Calhoun. John Calhoun, whose daughter she is supposed to have been, was born in Boston, Massachusetts, in either 1806 or 1808—both dates are given in different accounts. He came to Springfield, Illinois, in 1830, and on December 29 of the following year married Sarah Cutter. According to John Carroll Power's *History of the Early Settlers of Sangamon County, Illinois,* he had nine children, but among them a Sally or Sarah is not to be discovered.

However, it has been pointed out that the birth dates of two of Calhoun's children, as recorded in this volume, are three months apart; and it is argued that if his account is in error in this respect it is not unreasonable to doubt the infallibility of his list of the children's names. The fact remains, however, that in spite of this error—probably a printer's mistake—Power's *History* is a very reliable compilation, so reliable that it is constantly used by Springfield lawyers in the examination of abstracts, and readily accepted in court as furnishing satisfactory proof of heirship.

But the case against the existence of Sally rests on other evidence than Power's *History.* In a letter written from St. Joseph, Missouri, December 12, 1928, Mrs. Adele P. McCord, the only living grandchild of John Calhoun, stated: "I was an only grandchild on her side of the family & very fond of my Grandmother Sarah Cutter Calhoun. I became closely associated with her & my Aunts, and never once did I hear any of them called Sally." Mrs. McCord added that Mrs. Mary W. Inslee Kerr, of St. Joseph, Missouri, was the only person still alive who would have first-hand knowledge of the Calhoun family, and stated that she would get in touch with her if possible. In due time Mrs. Kerr's daughter answered on behalf of her mother, now ill. "General John Calhoun and his family," the letter reads, "were intimate friends of hers and there was never a daughter named, or called, Sally Calhoun."

2

Analysis of physical qualities and examination of the manner in which it was preserved are the only standards by which the Minor collection as a whole can be judged. In describing the outcome of tests other than these, it will be an advantage to divide the collection into several parts: (1) the Lincoln letters, (2) the books bearing Lincoln marginalia, (3) the Ann Rutledge letters, (4) Matilda Cameron's diary, and (5) Sally Calhoun's memoranda.

Since no unchallenged specimen of Ann Rutledge's writing is known to have been preserved, and since the very existence of Matilda Cameron and Sally Calhoun is at best doubtful, it is obvious that only the Lincoln letters and the books which he is supposed to have annotated can be judged on the score of handwriting. Yet the test is of the utmost significance. If the handwriting of the Lincoln documents in the Minor collection is indistinguishable from that of genuine Lincoln letters of the same approximate date, the presumption of authenticity is strong; but if it is markedly different, then all other flaws do no more than make the proof of spuriousness overwhelming.

Important as handwriting may be, however, there is little one can say about it. Actual comparison of specimens is the only test. Nevertheless, it may be worth while to point out one or two features of general appearance which can be reported in words. In the letters from the Minor collection Lincoln is frequently made to begin sentences with small letters. Letters of known authenticity never show this feature. Moreover, until the last few years of his life Lincoln usually— not always, of course—employed a short dash in place of a period. But in the Minor documents dashes are used only to indicate breaks—not terminations—of the thought.

In explaining the rakish, uneven appearance of the handwriting of these letters it has been argued that "Lincoln had two definitely distinct styles of writing his name—the formal signature, identified with legal documents or public business, and the more rambling and haphazard hand of friendly and familiar intercourse. The letters in this collection were of the second category. . . ."

This statement is true only to the extent that, in signing official papers as President, Lincoln usually wrote his name "Abraham Lincoln," while he signed letters of all descriptions with the familiar "A. Lincoln." Legal pleadings were generally signed "Lincoln, followed either by "p. q." (*pro querente*) or "p. d." (*pro defendant*). So far as the character of the handwriting is concerned, there is no distinction, beyond that due to a greater or lesser degree of haste, between that to be found in the body of the public and legal documents and that to be found in the body of letters.

It is true that not all specimens of Lincoln's writing are exactly similar, but the variations are the result of the writer's age rather than the character of the subject matter. Thus the handwriting of his youth shows immaturities not discernible in that of middle age, while letters written as President show clearly the effect of advancing age and mental strain. But the widest variations from these natural causes are as nothing compared with the difference between two intimate letters of the same approximate date, one from the Minor collection, the other indisputably genuine.

But in ruling out the Lincoln letters we need not depend on handwriting alone, conclusive as that should be. There is the evidence from "known character," so to speak. Does the Lincoln of the Minor letters harmonize with the Lincoln of historical fact? Or are they two different, distinct individuals—so different and distinct as not to be explained as variant phases of the same person?

In answering these questions I shall disregard, as being in the last analysis a matter of opinion, my belief that the distorted and unnatural individual pictured as the writer of the letters in the Minor collection does not square at all with the Lincoln of historical fact. Instead, I shall quote, for the reader's own comparison, two expressions on the same subject—slavery.

In one of the letters to John Calhoun, printed in the *Atlantic* for December 1928 (undated, but presumably written during his term in Congress), Lincoln is made to recount a conversation with a slave at the time of one of his two visits to New Orleans. Asked whether he was happy in slavery, the black had raised "a face of hopeless resignation" and answered, " 'No—no Marse I nevah is happy no mo. Whippins is things that black folks nevah can stop remembrin about—they hurt so.' " Lincoln then reminds his correspondent: "this is one I forgot to tell you before. but John I guess it takes a queer fellow like me to sympathise with the put upon and down trodden. those blacks John dont live—they simply *exist*. I never trapped an animal in my life and slavery to me is just *that* both filling my soul with abhorrence."

Compare the foregoing with the following extract from a letter to Mary Speed, the sister of the one man with whom Lincoln's intimacy is unquestioned. "By the way, a fine example was presented on board the boat [Lincoln was describing his return from a visit at the Speed home] for contemplating the effect of condition upon human happiness. A gentleman had purchased twelve negroes in different parts of Kentucky, and was taking them to a farm in the South. They were chained six and six together. . . . In this condition they were being separated forever from the scenes of their childhood, their friends, their fathers and mothers, and brothers and sisters, and many of them from their wives and children, and going into perpetual slavery, where the lash of the master is proverbially more ruthless and unrelenting than any other where; and yet amid all these distressing circumstances, as we would think them, they were the most cheerful and apparently happy creatures on board. One whose offense for which he had been sold was an over-fondness for his wife, played the fiddle almost continually, and the others danced, sang, cracked jokes, and played various games with cards from day to day. How true it is that 'God tempers the wind to the shorn lamb,' or in other words, that he renders the worst of human conditions tolerable, while he permits the best to be nothing better than tolerable."

It is only fair to point out that in 1855 Lincoln described this incident less amiably, calling slavery a "continued torment." My own belief is that this quickened perception of slavery's evil was a direct result of the agitation caused by the repeal of the Missouri Compromise in 1854. In any event, comparison of the two passages suggests, at least, the argument which could be built upon stylistic differences if space permitted. Is it possible for a man to write clear, easy prose in 1841, and seven years later to be guilty of verbiage resembling the stilted effort of a high-school freshman?

3

So much for the general character of the Minor letters from Lincoln in Washington to Calhoun in Springfield. The difference between the Lincoln of these letters and the Lincoln of historical fact is great enough to make a careful student skeptical, even if disquieting suspicions have not previously been aroused. And a skeptical student, if competent, will at once commence the most exacting, and most exciting, of all tests—the search for errors of specific fact.

The method consists in the critical examination of every fact which admits of independent verification. As this examination largely concerns John Calhoun and his relations with Lincoln, some comment upon him is necessary.

John Calhoun came to Springfield in 1830, and continued a resident of the town until his appointment as Surveyor–General of Kansas and Nebraska in 1854. From 1832 until 1835 he was Surveyor of Sangamon County. The county, then considerably larger than now, was being settled rapidly, and the demand for a surveyor's services was greater than one man could satisfy. At the instance of mutual friends Calhoun appointed Lincoln his deputy, with the specific duty of making surveys in the northwestern part of Sangamon County, now the separate county of Menard.

As time went on, Calhoun occupied other public offices. In 1838 he was elected to the legislature from Sangamon County. Four years later he was appointed Clerk of the Circuit Court and held the position until 1848, serving simultaneously as trustee of the defunct State Bank. As Lincoln advanced to a prominent position in local Whig circles, Calhoun gained place in the Democratic Party, becoming one of Douglas's trusted lieutenants when that leader rose to national prominence. Frequently Lincoln and Calhoun clashed in debate, and local tradition, well supported, has it that Lincoln feared no one, Douglas not excepted, more than Calhoun.

With these facts in mind, let us examine closely the letter of July 22, 1848. Aside from the fact that it implies a degree of political accord which did not exist, it contains several historical inconsistencies. "Jed was here and called on me about a month ago. he told me of your trip to Gentryville and your clearing the boundries, titles etc."—so Lincoln is made to write. Calhoun's trip must have taken place in 1848, or Lincoln, who took his seat in Congress in December 1847, would have known about it. But in 1848 Calhoun was Clerk of the Circuit Court, and the records show that he was performing the duties of that office in person. Relatively few legal papers for 1848 remain in the court files, but those that do contain his signature under the file date. Several were filed every month—frequently every week—during the entire year. For the month of May—the time most likely, according to the letter, for Calhoun to have made his Gentryville trip—the record is especially complete.

Moreover, even if Calhoun had gone to Gentryville, he could not have had for the reason of his visit that alleged in the letter. "He told me of your trip to Gentryville and your clearing the boundries, titles etc; Dear John at this time I want to extend my deepest gratitude for the service rendred my Mother," etc. The inference that Calhoun cleared "boundries, titles etc." for Lincoln's mother is inescapable. But in 1848 Lincoln's mother had no interest in any land at Gentryville. When Thomas Lincoln had removed from Kentucky to Indiana he entered one hundred and sixty acres near the present town of that name, but he never succeeded in obtaining a patent to more than eighty acres. This holding he sold to James Gentry in the winter of 1829–1830, shortly before removing to Illinois.

The last sentence of the letter is also open to suspicion. "Mary is well thank the Lord and joins in love to you and yours," Lincoln is supposed to have concluded. That Mrs. Lincoln was in Washington is a necessary inference. That she actually was in Washington is extremely doubtful. She had accompanied Lincoln there in the winter of 1847, but in the following spring she and the children had returned to the family home at Lexington, Kentucky. Her own letters show that she contemplated remaining there during July and August, and Lincoln's letters, particularly one dated July 2, show that he was fully conversant with her plans, and did not expect her to join him soon. There is no direct evidence of Mrs. Lincoln's movements from early July until mid-October, but all the information accessible indicates that her presence in Washington on July 22, 1848, is highly improbable.

So much for the letter of July 22, 1848. That to Calhoun of May 9, 1834, offers even greater inconsistencies, one in particular admitting no explanation of any sort. "There seems some controversy," Lincoln writes, "between him and Green concerning that North East quarter of Section 40—you remember?" Since 1785 the government system of surveys had provided for townships divided into thirty–six sections, numbered consecutively from one to thirty–six. Natural irregularities occasionally resulted in townships with fewer than thirty–six sections, but never in one with more than that number. For Lincoln to have inquired of Calhoun—both men being official surveyors—regarding a "Section 40" is unthinkable.

In the same letter Lincoln remarks that "the 'Bixbys' are leaving this week for some place in Kansas." Kansas, however, was not open for white settlement until twenty years after the date of this letter. A few squatters, guides, and Indian traders were clustered about its military posts at an earlier date, but that was all. It is doubtful whether even the word "Kansas" was in common use as designating the region it now describes. Most maps of the period referred to describe the vast territory west of Missouri and north of Arkansas Territory simply as "Missouri Territory" or "Indian Territory," while the gazetteers list the word only as the name of a river.

4

The books bearing Lincoln marginalia in the Minor collection are no more worthy of credence than the letters. The handwriting is equally unlike that which is indisputably his. In addition, there is no indication that Lincoln was in the habit of underlining and commenting upon passages in the books he owned. Many books from his library are in existence, but not one whose authenticity is above suspicion contains any writing other than his name or a simple presentation inscription.

Moreover, no reliance need be placed upon these general considerations to prove spurious the notations in at least one of the volumes of the collection. This is Newman's *Practical System of Rhetoric,* containing many underscorings and comments. The book was published in 1829 at Andover, Massachusetts. On the flyleaf is the name of its original owner: "Miss Susan Y. Baker, March 15 Eastport Academy." At the bottom of the title-page is the signature, "A. Lincoln; Gentryville." At the top of the page, in the same handwriting, are a few lines expressing gratitude to Miss Baker for her gift of the book. All seems regular enough (the handwriting always excepted) until one discovers that the preface of the book is dated, in type, May 1829. Consequently Miss Baker's inscription, "March 15," could not have been written earlier than 1830. And on March 15, 1830, Abraham Lincoln was not residing in Indiana, having, according to his own statement, departed for Illinois some two weeks before that time.

When these specific discrepancies are added to the evidence of spuriousness which the examination of handwriting, general content, and documentary history amassed, proof becomes overwhelming. No matter what the character of the rest of the collection, the Lincoln documents are worthless.

The other items in the Minor collection contain even more historical inconsistencies than the Lincoln material. Two grave errors are to be found in the Ann Rutledge letters alone.

Twice Ann refers to the New Salem schoolmaster as "Newton Graham." The name, in fact, was Mentor Graham. In the Illinois State Historical Library are poll books for the year 1834 signed Mentor Graham. In the Menard County records at Petersburg, Illinois, are several legal documents in which the name is given as Mentor Graham; and Mrs. Henry Bradley, a granddaughter living at Greenview, Illinois, has two deeds and three promissory notes so signed. Moreover, Mrs. Bradley, who knew Graham before his death, never heard him called by any other name than Mentor. Her recollection is supported by several other members of the family who were in close contact with him for several years, and who also state that they never knew of his using any other name than Mentor.

More conclusive, however, than a mistake in a name is the following sentence from one of Ann's letters to Lincoln. "I am greatfull," the writer says, "for the Spencers copy-book I copy frum that every time I can spair." Since Ann Rutledge died on August 25, 1835,—the date is recorded in the family Bible,—this letter was written prior to that time. But Spencer's first publication on penmanship, under the title of Spencer and Rice's *System of Business and Ladies' Penmanship,* was not issued until 1848.

It has been suggested, nevertheless, that although Spencer's first formal treatise on penmanship was not published until 1848 he might have been issuing copy books or leaflets many years before that time, all trace of which has since disappeared. As a matter of fact, the work here mentioned was not a formal treatise, but exactly the sort of publication contemplated in the suggestion I have stated. It consisted of small slips of paper with mottoes lithographed in Spencerian writing, each packet of slips being enclosed in a long envelope similar to those in ordinary use to-day.

I have already referred, in connection with the question of whether or not Matilda Cameron was a real person, to one grave error in her diary. There are others. Twice she writes of boats from Springfield. On July 10, 1833, she states that her church got the first *Missouri Harmony Hymn Book* "last boat from Springfield"; while a later entry records that "the boat being du Satiday cum in while we wuz by the mill." Both references indicate plainly that boats carrying passengers were running between Springfield and New Salem on a regular schedule.

To anyone familiar with the Sangamon River, and the

country through which it passes, the idea is absurd. The river swings around Springfield in a rough semicircle, coming no nearer than five miles at any point. Besides, it is called a "river" more by courtesy than because the size of the stream merits the description. Generally it is no larger than a good-sized creek, and in July—when, according to Matilda, boats were running regularly—it will hardly float a canoe. Moreover, it meanders from Springfield to New Salem in wide curves, probably running a course of fifty miles between the two towns, less than twenty miles distant by air line. Under these circumstances, a packet line was simply impossible.

Lincoln's published correspondence reveals a second flaw in the Cameron diary. One of Matilda's boats—the one which was "du Satiday"—brought "Dave turnham a frend of Abes from gentryville" to New Salem. This was the same Turnham to whom Lincoln, on October 23, 1860, wrote a letter in which the following statement occurs: "I well remember when you and I last met, after a separation of fourteen years, at the cross-road voting place in the fall of 1844." Thus we have Lincoln's own word that he had not seen Turnham from the time he left Indiana in 1830 until he made a campaign trip to the vicinity of his old home in the fall of 1844.

Another entry in the diary commences with the statement, "Marthy Calhone teeched Ann sum new patern of kroshay and she is going to tech me." This entry must have been dated 1835 or earlier, yet Martha Calhoun, sixth child of John Calhoun, was not born until January 9, 1843. This somewhat startling weakness in chronology has been explained on the ground that Calhoun had a sister Martha, to whom the reference might naturally apply. The explanation is possible, of course, but very unlikely. In the first place, if Calhoun's sister Martha was living with him she would not have been at New Salem,—a misapprehension which runs through all these documents,—but at Springfield. In the second place, Calhoun's father was a prosperous Eastern merchant, well able to support his family. It hardly seems likely that a young woman would have left a comfortable home in an established community for the hardships of life in a raw Illinois village.

One more observation, and we are done with Matilda Cameron. Her final diary entry, dated March 12, 1836, contains the following statement: "sum folks has left Sand Ridge and also a lot in Salem. . . . John Calhone and family has al-reddy gone. Abe is tendin surveying for him hear what litle ther is to do." The statement contains two errors of fact. Never having lived in New Salem, John Calhoun of course had not migrated. In 1836, as for the past six years, he was living in Springfield. And whatever surveying Lincoln was doing was for Thomas M. Neale, not Calhoun, who had resigned his position the previous year. I have not been able to find the exact date of of Calhoun's resignation, but as early as September 26, 1835, Neale was signing surveys as Surveyor of Sangamon County.

Only the memoranda of Sally Calhoun remain. Several of the objections raised against the other documents apply here with equal force—this failure of the picture of Lincoln there drawn to harmonize with his known character, the improbability of an interest in Lincoln great enough to have led Calhoun to dictate these reminiscences, the frequent use of the name "Newton Graham." Most important, however, is the fact that the memoranda, dated St. Joseph, Missouri, imply the presence of Calhoun, although Calhoun—be it insisted yet once more—was still living in Springfield. It is useless to cite evidence proving that Calhoun was actually in Springfield on certain dates, for only one of Sally's memoranda is dated. That one was supposedly written on June 2, 1848. On May 29 Calhoun put his file mark and signature on legal papers in Springfield, and it was practically impossible for him to have been in St. Joseph four days later. Even if, by strenuous traveling, he had succeeded in making the trip in that time, it is straining credulity too far to believe that he would at once have put his daughter to recording incidents in the early life of Lincoln.

5

Thus every test except that of the fitness of the paper has found the Minor collection defective. Critical examination showed glaring weaknesses in the line according to which the collection is supposed to have descended. The handwriting of the items which purport to have been written by Lincoln bears no resemblance to that of authentic documents. The content of the Lincoln letters is not in complete harmony with his known ideas on one subject at least, slavery, and it is difficult to believe that such wide stylistic differences as have been pointed out can occur in the writing of the same individual. And the number of historical inconsistencies, some of which admit no possible explanation, is very large. By no possibility can the Minor collection be genuine.

Then who fabricated it? We know what sort of person the forger was, for in these documents he has drawn the outlines of his own character. Considerable cleverness dictated the explanation of the collection's formation and descent to the present. The character of Matilda Cameron, exceedingly well drawn, indicates no small degree of creative ability. Wide though superficial reading provided enough information about Lincoln's life to deceive those whose knowledge was not fairly extensive. Only when cleverness, artistic skill, and general information could no longer suffice, and sound knowledge became indispensable, did the forger fail. Certainly he—or she—was not familiar with Lincoln's correspondence, either in its original or in its published form. Complete ignorance of the geographical setting of the story was coupled with defective knowledge of the minor characters. Under the circumstances it was only natural that the forger, like an amateur playwright, should overdraw his Lincoln, emphasizing too strongly his best-known traits.

That exposure followed quickly should cause no regret, for the Lincoln of the Minor collection was, after all, a sorry character. What he wrote was full of inflated sentimentality, and the manner in which he wrote it suggested a man no more than half literate. To me, at least, a belief in the common authorship of these documents and the Gettysburg Address was impossible—and I much prefer the Gettysburg Address.

A Shelf
of Lincoln Books

Twenty-five or thirty years ago I came to the conclusion
that much of the great mass of Lincoln literature was
trivial, repetitive, or just plain worthless. I decided to make
a selection that would be quite adequate for a public or
college library. The result was *A Shelf of Lincoln Books.* I
think that the book had value at the time, but that it is now
outdated.

Not so with the Introduction, I hope. I could have stated
my purpose in a paragraph like the foregoing, but my
good friend George W. Bunn, Jr., of Springfield, Illinois,
whose advice on literary matters has been of incomparable
value to me, said: "You should go further. Tell your
readers why they should read about Lincoln, or, for that
matter, anybody out of the past." Which is what I tried to
do here.

In introducing this little book I could content myself with
the summary statement of a few obvious truths. I could
point to the great bulk of Lincoln literature,* and let readers
themselves draw one sure inference—namely, that few stu-

From *A Shelf of Lincoln Books,* by Paul M. Angle, 1946, by courtesy
of Rutgers University Press

*Jay Monaghan, in *Lincoln Bibliography, 1839–1939,* lists 3,958 books
and pamphlets which are concerned in major part with Lincoln's life.
No satisfactory bibliography of Lincoln articles in periodicals has been
compiled, but the number of such articles certainly runs into four
figures. And there are thousands of books which deal significantly,
though not primarily, with Lincoln's career.

dents and fewer librarians have time to winnow the permanent from the inconsequential. I could show that many Lincoln books were little better than worthless when they were published, and that many others, good enough in their time, have lost much of the value they once possessed. I could demonstrate that many of those who have written about Lincoln had little equipment for the task except interest in the subject, and that in consequence Lincoln literature must be approached with more than usual caution. And thus I would have achieved the justification which every author who adds another Lincoln book considers obligatory.

These are, of course, valid reasons for a selective, critical bibliography, and most readers will find them sufficient. I hope, however, that there will be some who will be moved by a further reason that led me to undertake the writing of this book. I have found pleasure, interest, and I believe some enlightenment in knowing more than casually a great man and the period in which he lived, and I hope that this book will lead others to a similar reward.

Some years ago I met a man who was only a little short of one hundred years of age. He was the leading citizen of the town in which he lived, and still active in his law practice and several commercial enterprises. We talked about the great depression which had followed the crash of 1929. It had been bad, very bad, he admitted, but he had never lost heart. He remembered too many others—'57, '73, '93, and so on for almost a century. He had perspective. Few of us can count on achieving that quality by the accident of exceptional longevity, but vicarious experience is ours for the effort—and usually the pleasurable effort—of acquiring it.

For example. The country, you will hear it said, is going to hell at high speed. A short time ago I read a letter in which the writer proclaimed to his correspondent that he was "extremely mortified at our public proceedings; it appears to me that real Insanity has taken possession of mens minds." That was written in 1795,* and I suppose similar letters

*The writer was John Langdon, of Portsmouth, N.H., one of the signers of the Constitution of the United States. The letter is in the collection of the Chicago Historical Society.

have been written, or similar sentiments expressed, ever since men began to live together. The tragedy is that so many people not only believe in incipient calamity, but act impulsively on the belief. Thus we have a Ku Klux Klan to combat the menace of the Roman Catholic Church and the foreignborn, a Father Coughlin to lead a crusade against Jews and communists. Given the perspective that comes from knowledge of the past—from knowledge, in this instance, of the rise and disintegration of the Know Nothing Party, of the sorry fate of the original Klan, of the Red scare of the early Twenties, of Jewish contributions to American life—and fewer men would lose their heads. That, at any rate, is my conviction.

This is not to say, of course, that the historical perspective does or should blind one to danger signals. But it should serve as a brake on impulse. He who possesses it is likely to ask whether what seems to be a sign of danger really is one, and insist on some evidence beyond mere mass conviction. Balance, rather than blindness, is its genuine and beneficial product.

Then there are the myriad lights which the past throws on the present. Who can begin to understand the attitude of Southern politicians towards the poll tax without knowing something of the Civil War and Reconstruction? Can anyone come to sound conclusions regarding the Negro problem unless he is familiar with the place the Negro has occupied in the American social fabric for at least the last century? How account for our curious and contradictory attitude towards Great Britain, for our puzzling mixture of friendliness and suspicion, without knowledge of many phases of American history—our national origins, our wars, our diplomacy, our German and Irish heritage? How can one understand our reluctance to adopt universal military service unless he knows our military history?

But these are utilitarian values. By their means history may lead to wisdom, although one would probably be hard put to show that historians, as a class, rank much above their fellowmen in their possession of that unusual virtue. There can be no doubt, however, about the fact that to a large number of its devotees history affords both interest and pleasure. The man who knows the past thoroughly can hardly help living a richer, more interesting life than the man to whom the past is only a dark void.

To illustrate the point, I submit one or two homely, personal illustrations. For a dozen years I lived in a house that faced what was once the fair grounds of Sangamon County, Illinois. The tract has long been devoted to ordinary urban uses, so that residences, small apartments, a public school, a Catholic academy and convent now stand there. But when I sat on my porch in the dark quiet of late summer evenings I could see more than a row of houses across the street. I could see thousands of delirious Republicans jamming those grounds one August day in 1860, hear the speakers shouting the praises of Old Abe Lincoln, and watch Lincoln himself barely escape from the cheering, crushing crowd when he made a personal appearance. I could look on as hundreds of Illinois farm boys stumbled through the manual of arms when Camp Yates was located on the old fair grounds in the spring of 1861. I could see, in my mind's eye, an undistinguished little man with reddish brown hair and a short beard assume command of the 21st Illinois Infantry, and I knew what none of those who were there at the time could have guessed—that in four years he was to receive Lee's surrender at Appomattox, and in four years more he was to take the presidential oath of office from the steps of the United States Capitol. Somehow, what I could bring from the past made living there richer by far than it would have been had I been able to see nothing but my neighbors' homes.

As I write these lines I look over Michigan Avenue to Grant Park, and beyond it, Lake Michigan. From the avenue come the muffled roar of automobile engines and the swish of tires; beyond it a suburban train is passing; on the lake a regatta is in progress. But I can look down from my window and blot out one of the world's most famous streets and the park that lies beyond it. Where the traffic now moves in an endless line I can see the old lake shore, with the lake itself lying still as glass on a sultry August morning. I watch a straggling procession moving south along the beach—some Indians on horseback, a company of soldiers, women and children in wagons at the rear. And I know that only a mile or so farther on death will come to most of them in the Fort Dearborn massacre. My view, absorbing as it is today, takes on another dimension from the past.

And one can do more, with a thorough knowledge of a segment of the past, than conjure up imaginary pictures. He can create a world into which he can slip at will, and for a man to have a retreat which no one else can penetrate is good for his soul. Suppose one's world is the England of Charles II. In his library, after a day in the hard and troublesome world of 1946, he can take the place, if he will, of Samuel Pepys. He can stand in awe while the Great Fire destroys hundreds of acres of his beloved London, catch a glimpse of the beauteous but wicked Nell Gwynne, and if he be so minded, indulge—with complete impunity—in peccadilloes which he neither could nor would permit himself in real life. He can live in another age—see its sights, hear its sounds, smell its smells, think its thoughts. He will come to know a great number of people whom it will be good to know—the clever, cynical, amusing king; his courtiers and mistresses; fellow-diarists like John Evelyn; John Dryden, poet and dramatist; the Earl of Clarendon, statesman and historian; and a host of actors and actresses, musicians, servant girls, and shady characters who are likely to be even more interesting than the great men and women of the time.

From such an experience, repeated effortlessly, he cannot fail to profit. His excursions into other times will often be almost as rejuvenating as his actual vacation trips. He will have the great satisfaction that comes from knowing anything thoroughly. He will be able to correct, from his own sure knowledge, much misinformation that he will encounter, and for the remainder of his life he will be healthily skeptical of the printed page. He will find himself endowed with new understanding, greater tolerance, and more humility.

Any period in history offers these rewards. One can make a case for the Age of Pericles or the Rome of Augustus, for Shakespeare's England or Samuel Johnson's, for the France of Louis XIV or the French Revolution, for the Italian

Renaissance, for the Ireland of George Moore, Synge, and Yeats, to name only a few. Not many periods, however, can approach in their potentialities the United States in the time of Abraham Lincoln. The advantages of that period are many. First among them, perhaps, is the geographical scope of Lincoln's life. An average American interested in Anthony Trollope will be fortunate to visit "Barsetshire" once in his lifetime. That same American, interested in Lincoln, will have many opportunities for experiencing that feeling of intimacy that comes from standing in places where a man of the past actually lived. Kentucky, Indiana, Illinois, and Washington by no means exhaust the places associated with Lincoln's life. Iowa, Kansas, Missouri, Wisconsin, Michigan, and Ohio treasure the memory of his visits; Massachusetts, Pennsylvania, New Jersey, and Virginia are proud of having harbored his ancestors. Moreover, if one extends his interest beyond Lincoln biography to the Civil War, there is hardly a locality in the eastern half of the country without its associations.

In the second place, the extensive literature that makes a book of this kind desirable is itself a good reason for choosing Lincoln as a subject. The materials for knowing the man and his time are readily available. Many of the books described in the following pages are on the shelves of every good-sized public library, and with the exception of a dozen titles, all can be purchased from the publishers or from antiquarian booksellers for modest sums. No real enthusiast, however, will confine himself to this list. Before long he will discover that *The Diary of Orville Hickman Browning,* not included here, throws lights of rare quality on Lincoln's life. If he becomes interested in Browning, the chances are that he will find his way sooner or later to Usher F. Linder's inimitable *Reminiscences of the Early Bench and Bar of Illinois.* Linder may lead to Ford's *History of Illinois,* and that, perhaps, to a neglected American classic, the *Memoirs of Gustave Koerner.* The direction of one's tangential interests makes little difference. Lincoln's associates, his background, the Civil War—on these and all related subjects the books exist, and anyone can find them easily.

Lincoln's associates, by the way, offer a particularly fascinating field for study. Most Americans have a hazy recollection from school history days of Seward, Stanton, Cameron, Welles, Chase, and a few of the best known military leaders. If they remember anything, they remember stereotypes—the dynamic Stanton, who organized the armies and people of the North for victory; the cool, capable, incorruptible Chase, who financed the war; the vacillating McClellan who almost lost it; and so forth. But when they get beneath the surface of history the stereotypes vanish and they find themselves in the midst of hot argument. Was Stanton really capable, or was he only a cowardly tyrant who made himself a reputation by bluster and rudeness? Or worse? Chase incorruptible? In the financial sense, yes, but what did his ambition do to his moral fibre? McClellan vacillating? As soon as one passes his novitiate in Civil War history he encounters a school of students who hold that McClellan was the North's greatest commander! Before long, one comes to know these men almost as friends and enemies.

The Lincoln period, moreover, has the advantage of not being so remote in time that one has to strain to find connections with the present. One takes the Alton Railroad from Chicago to Springfield, and realizes that that road, like most of the other main lines that now serve the Middle West, was begun in the last decade of Lincoln's career at the Illinois bar. If he chooses the Illinois Central for the same trip, he will be traveling on a road which for several years retained Lincoln as one of its attorneys. The steel plow and the reaper, still basic in agriculture, came into existence in his maturity. The factory system had just begun to displace handcraftsmen, at least in the Old Northwest, when he assumed the presidency. And centralization in government, which remains one of our most crucial problems, is generally connected with his administration.

But the best of all reasons for studying Lincoln's life is the fact that he was a truly great man. He not only influenced the course of history; he also exemplified those virtues to which civilized man has given his highest allegiance—steadfastness, faith in righteousness, humility, and the forgiving spirit. At the same time his humor, his earthiness, his utter lack of pretension made him one with common humanity. To spend time—much time—in such a man's company can be one of life's privileges.

Introduction to
Abraham Lincoln:
Speeches and Letters

I include this short biographical sketch and evaluation
because it was directed toward English readers, and
therefore has a special flavor (or flavour?).

On the 12th February 1809 Abraham Lincoln was born
in a log cabin in a sparsely settled region of Kentucky. Later
in that same year William E. Gladstone was born in a
comfortable home in the thriving city of Liverpool.

At that time no one, either in the United States or in
England, would have been rash enough to predict that
fifty–two years later both Lincoln and Gladstone would be
leaders of their respective people, the one as a newly elected
President, the other as the dominant figure in the English
cabinet.

Yet in the case of Gladstone the prediction would not
have been a wild one. His father was a man of large fortune
who sat in Parliament for many years. The son would have
the best school and university education which family position
and wealth could procure. He would not need to earn a
living, and could devote all his time and energy to public
life.

The parents of Abraham Lincoln, on the other hand, were
poor pioneers, though no poorer than most of their neigh-
bours. The father could barely read and write, the mother
made her mark. The boy would grow to maturity on back-
woods farms and would learn no more in the makeshift
schools that the region offered than to read, write, and do

From the book *Abraham Lincoln: Speeches and Letters,* ed. by Paul M.
Angle. Everyman's Library Edition. Published by E. P. Dutton & Co.,
Inc., and used with their permission

simple arithmetic. After striking out on his own he would earn his living as a clerk in a frontier store, as village postmaster, and as a surveyor of the virgin lands that new settlers were then taking up.

Even after Lincoln was well advanced in life he gave no sign of future greatness. He served four terms in the state legislature, but hundreds of other men were also members of that body. During his one term in Congress he did not distinguish himself, and had he run again he could not have been re-elected. In the practice of the law—for which he had trained himself—he stood well, but no one would have included him among the eminent American lawyers of his time.

At forty–five he had been inactive in politics for several years. But in the year in which he attained that age—1854—the Kansas–Nebraska Act was passed. The effect of the bill was to open federal territories, not yet organized as states, to slavery. Lincoln, aroused as never before, re-entered politics and did all that was within his power to repeal the new legislation. Out of the opposition of thousands like him the Republican Party came into existence. Within two years he was its acknowledged leader in Illinois.

In 1858 Stephen A. Douglas, Senator from Illinois, stood for re-election. Lincoln was the unanimous choice of his party to oppose the man who, as sponsor of the Kansas–Nebraska Act, personified the policy it represented. In the ensuing campaign Lincoln, though unsuccessful, won a nation-wide hearing and earned a national reputation. Two years later the Republican National Convention chose him as its presidential nominee. With the Democrats divided, he won the election.

Lincoln took office on 4th March 1861, an untried man. He had had legislative experience; he possessed a logical mind and the ability to reduce complex issues to simple terms; yet there had been nothing in his life to prepare him for the ordeal he faced. He rose to the challenge magnificently, and guided the nation through four years of war precipitated by the South's determined attempt to secede from the Union.

And at the same time that he was burdened almost beyond endurance by cares that furrowed his face and wore down his rail-splitter's iron physique, he wrote some of the most sublime prose to be found in the English language. The totality of Lincoln's truly great writing is not large. It would include, when measured by the severest standards, perhaps only the Gettysburg Address in its entirety, a half-dozen letters, and passages in other speeches, notably the first and second inaugural addresses. But of what other writers, devoting their lives to the creation of pure literature, can much more be said? And who, at his best, has surpassed the finest work of this man who never completely mastered the niceties of composition, who read almost nothing?

Even below the summit of achievement, Lincoln's writing has compelling interest. Except for a short-lived venture into verse and the story of a bizarre incident from his early years at the Bar, he wrote only for utilitarian purposes. Most of his letters were those of a practising lawyer, a politician, a high government official. Disregarding two or three lectures, he made speeches in the same capacities. Although there were certainly times when he consciously strove for effect, on the whole he sought merely to make himself understood, and, when the situation warranted, to convince. Yet this workaday prose exhibits a style simple, direct, terse, which can also be imaginative and metaphorical. If two sentences would cover Lincoln's purpose he wrote two sentences, but he did not subscribe to the fallacy that any short letter is better than a long one. If he needed four pages to develop an argument he took four pages, just as he did not hesitate to make a speech of three hours' duration. Few writers have ever advanced ideas with more severe logic. (Whether he derived the logical habit of thought from his study of Euclid, or whether an innately logical mind aroused his interest in Euclid, is an open question.) And always, in his prose, there is clarity—clarity in such high degree that only in the rarest instances does one have to read a sentence a second time in order to comprehend its exact meaning.

Still, if the criterion were solely literary, public interest would hardly support even a limited compilation of Lincoln's writings. But the criterion can never be solely literary. What Lincoln wrote is indispensable to an understanding of the man. The strictly autobiographical documents are few, brief, and incomplete, but they supply facts that could have been established only with great difficulty, if at all, from other sources. Much more important is the light which Lincoln's letters and speeches shed upon his character, personality, and the quality of his mind. Often a casual letter discloses a trait more convincingly than the commentary of long-time associates and friends. He was honest, his contemporaries have said, but their testimony has had to do with the kind of honesty that leads a store-keeper to return an overcharge, that impels a lawyer to take scrupulous care of his clients' money. What of that greater, rarer quality that induces a politician to state his convictions with complete candour, even though he courts defeat by doing so? No one who follows Lincoln's course on the Mexican war, or reads his speeches in the debates with Douglas even as they are abridged in this volume, can doubt that here was a man who valued integrity above success. What of those human qualities so universally admired, so uncommonly practised—patience, humility, sympathy for the unfortunate and sorrow-stricken, gentleness of spirit? That these were attributes of Lincoln is abundantly proved by letters to hot-tempered friends, to ungenerous critics, to young men discouraged by initial failures, to parents and relatives of soldiers killed in battle. What of his conception of moral values? His whole discussion of the slavery question reveals one for whom no sophistry could cloud the distinction between right and wrong; who also, knowing that distinction, would stand unwaveringly on what he considered right. Yet his mind was such that while he could know the right as it concerned relations between men, he could only grope for it as it existed between men and God. But here too his writings show him to have been either a deeply religious man or—unthinkably—an unconscionable hypocrite.

These qualities and characteristics of Abraham Lincoln are aspects of the image which millions of his countrymen have shared ever since his death. Other traits, also exemplified in his writings, the general public has chosen either to ignore or to minimize. He had ambition. For more than thirty years he sought election to office without attempting to dissemble his desires, yet many continue to picture him as one who, but for the urging of his friends, would have effaced himself in the practice of the law. He was patient with imposition, but he was not supine. In any personal relationship there came a point on which he would not yield—a point which patrons of his post office, political opponents, generals, and finally the people of the South, discovered to their consternation. Occasionally he became testy, and sometimes at small irritations; less frequently he blazed with anger.

This is only to say that Lincoln was human, and therefore within the comprehension of ordinary mortals. And it is important that he be understood. He had greatness, and to know greatness is one of life's highest privileges. Moreover, without an understanding of Lincoln one can have no more than an imperfect grasp of the course of the United States for the past century, and cannot fully know the nation as it is to-day. As the Civil War recedes in time, it assumes ever larger importance as the paramount event in the last one hundred years of American life. For the United States, the war accelerated industrialism in the east and north and retarded it in the south, gave a tremendous impetus to centralization in government, produced cleavages between sections that have influenced every national election since 1865, and created a racial problem which the passage of time gives little promise of solving. For the world, it proved that democracy, as a form of government, had come to stay.

The focal figure of the Civil War was Abraham Lincoln. In the span of his adult life the forces that would lead to conflict gathered and reached the breaking point. William Lloyd Garrison brought out the first number of the *Liberator* advocating the abolition of slavery less than a year after Lincoln came of age. In six years the pro-slavery reaction would be so violent that Lincoln had to face it in the Illinois legislature. After the passage of the Kansas–Nebraska Act he would think out the issues, debate them, clarify them for millions. In his speeches up to and including the first

Inaugural Address the points of difference over which the American people would shed blood are expounded with superlative clarity.

Once war came, it was Lincoln who defined both its purpose and significance so persuasively as to hold the adherence of the vast majority of the American people. Not only that: it was Lincoln who made the critical decisions—against premature emancipation, for emancipation when the time was ripe, in favour of relieving one commander and selecting another, for certain strategical concepts in preference to others, for a kind of reconstruction that would reunite the nation in spirit as well as actuality. What he did, and why he did what he did, can be fully understood only from the record which he himself created.

A final point needs to be made. The record that Lincoln created—his letters, his speeches, his memoranda, his homilies—was his alone. Four documents in this volume—the letters to Queen Victoria and the King of Siam, the proclamations calling out the militia and designating a day of thanksgiving—were probably prepared in the State Department. All others sprang directly from Lincoln's own mind.

The Lincoln Funeral

Influenced by the account of the Lincoln funeral in Lloyd
Lewis's fine book, *Myths After Lincoln,* I started out to make
this a set piece. My first draft ran to thirty pages at least. I
was not happy with it, nor was I happy with the result of
minor tinkerings. I finally decided that the way to handle
the subject was with the utmost brevity and restraint, so in
the end thirty pages came down to two pages. And I was
satisfied.

In the small hours of April 15th Springfield learned the
tragic news. At three o'clock in the morning, amid despatches
from Grant's army in Richmond, accounts of Lee's surrender,
and New York gold quotations, came the first terse flash
from Washington: "The President was shot in a theatre
tonight, and is probably mortally wounded." By dawn it was
known that death was only a matter of hours.

In sadness and anxiety the people gathered in groups
on the streets. A few stores which had opened for business
closed, and the quiet of a Sunday prevailed. Flags flew at
half-mast, buildings were draped with black cloth, church
bells tolled. At eight o'clock came word of Lincoln's death.
Four hours later the citizens met in the State House and
listened to John T. Stuart speak of the dead President.
That afternoon one organization after another—the Union
League, the Fenian Brotherhood, the City Council—met to
give formal expression to the sorrow which all men felt.

The next day, a Sunday, the churches were crowded, and

From *"Here I Have Lived": A History of Lincoln's Springfield, 1821-1865,*
by Paul M. Angle, The Abraham Lincoln Association, Springfield,
Ill., 1935, pp. 290–92

ministers decried the national calamity from black-draped pulpits. On the 19th, when funeral services were held in Washington, stores and offices were again closed; again flags hung at half-mast. At noon the guns at the arsenal fired a solemn salute; that afternoon there were services in all the churches. It was another day of sadness and mourning.

By this time preparations for the funeral were under way. In Washington, on the 17th, an Illinois delegation had secured Mrs. Lincoln's consent to the burial of the body in Springfield. At the same time a local committee had been chosen to make arrangements for an appropriate site for the grave. Soon afterward, with unanimous approval from the city, the Mather property* was chosen, and the construction of a temporary tomb commenced. Then, just as the vault was completed, word came from Mrs. Lincoln that the body was to be deposited in the receiving vault at Oak Ridge. The people were disappointed, but the committee acceded to her wish.

Meanwhile, the funeral train had been slowly moving westward. In Philadelphia, New York, Cleveland, Indianapolis and other cities hundreds of thousands had looked upon the features of the dead President. On the first of May the cortege reached Chicago, where the body was to lie for twenty-four hours. On the third it would be in Springfield.

The day broke bright and clear. Dawn found the streets crowded—for hours special trains had been pouring thousands into the prairie capital. By eight o'clock the Alton station was an island in a human sea, and other thousands lined the tracks beyond the limits of the town. The 146th Illinois, with detachments from other regiments, was drawn up in line on Jefferson street. Minute guns, fired by a Missouri battery, sounded strangely sharp against the hushed voices of the crowd.

Shortly before nine o'clock the pilot engine arrived. A strained silence was the crowd's only manifestation. A few minutes later the funeral train, nine black-draped cars, drew slowly into the station. In absolute quiet the body was placed

---

*The site of the present State House.

in the magnificent hearse which the city of St. Louis had tendered for the occasion, and the long procession started for the State House. There, in the Hall of the House of Representatives, the coffin was placed on a velvet-covered catafalque. The guard of honor took their places, the casket was opened, and the people started to file past. All day and all night the slow procession continued, until it was said that 75,000 had looked upon the face of Lincoln.

At ten o'clock on the morning of May 4th the coffin was closed. While minute guns sounded, and a choir of 250 voices sang hymns on the State House steps, the casket was placed in the hearse. With Genral Hooker at its head, the long procession started towards Oak Ridge. The cemetery reached, the choir sang again while the body was placed in the tomb. A minister offered a prayer, another read scripture, a third read the Second Inaugural. The choir sang a dirge, and Bishop Simpson pronounced the funeral oration. There was a closing prayer, the Doxology, a benediction. Slowly, silently, the vast crowd dispersed.

Tragic Years: The Civil War and its Commemoration

I was angry when I wrote this diatribe against the tawdry commercialization of the Civil War centennial. A dozen years later I am still angry, and I see no reason to apologize for any part of what I wrote. The subject might be considered out of date, but I think it has timeliness because of the approaching bicentennial of the American Revolution.

Four years ago the Congress of the United States, by joint resolution, established the Civil War Centennial Commission, consisting of twenty-five members, and charged it with the responsibility of preparing a general plan for commemorating the one-hundredth anniversary of the Civil War. In due course General U. S. Grant III, grandson of the original Ulysses, was chosen chairman. While General Grant has by no means been idle, the real mainspring of the Commission has been and is, Mr. Karl S. Betts, executive director.

From the beginning, the Commission has sought to stimulate other organizations to conduct centennial observances, and to coordinate their activities, rather than to mount a program of its own. In this it has been remarkably successful. Forty-odd states now have Civil War centennial commissions of their own, although there were only thirty-six states at the time of the war, and all kinds of private groups—historical

From the *South Atlantic Quarterly*, Autumn 1961, pp. 375–89. Copyright 1961 by the Duke University Press societies, Civil War Round Tables—have been prodded into action. The Commission's goals, as offically defined, are admirable. I quote a statement published on August 22, 1958:

> To commemorate the centennial of this war we do not want simply to string together a series of holidays, reviving here the exultation of victory and there the sadness of defeat. Rather, the centennial must give us a new understanding of the way in which Americans built from sacrifice and suffering an enduring Nation and a lasting peace. . . .
>
> The centennial observance must be a new study of American patriotism—a study which should give us a deeper understanding of the immense reserves of bravery, of sacrifice, and of idealism which lie in the American character.

The *Official Guide for the Observance of the Centennial of the Civil War,* a Commission publication, stresses memorial observances, the preservation of historical materials, educational activities, and publications. The *Guide* goes further, and warns against re-enactment of battles and historical pageants on the sound ground that they are likely to be travesties.

But the temptation to lick the Yanks a second time in a hundred years proved to be irresistible. Plans were made to re-enact the fall of Fort Sumter, and after that the battles of Lexington (Missouri), First Bull Run, Antietam, and Brice's Cross Roads, as well as Van Dorn's raid on Holly Springs. These, of course, are projects of the state Civil War commissions for which the national commission cannot be held responsible, although one can detect a certain degree of gratification in the Commission's reporting of the plans.

It should have been great fun to bang away at Fort Sumter. That was one engagement of the Civil War that could have been staged with a high degree of fidelity. In 1861 the fort and the shore batteries in Charleston harbor exchanged shots for thirty-six hours and produced one casualty—a horse on Morris Island. But this idyllic prospect—the re-enactment of a battle in which no one was more than inconvenienced— faded out. The show was to have coincided with a meeting of the Civil War Centennial Commission to which all the state commissions had been invited. Charleston hotelkeepers, discovering that this meant lodging for a few Negroes from the Northern states, announced that the "White Only" sign would be hanging out as usual. Five state commissions announced that they would stay home. The national Commission hurriedly hunted up quarters at the nearby United States Navel Base, where no color line is drawn. It was compelled to announce, however, that men and women would have to be housed separately. So sexual segregation was substituted for racial segregation. Is this progress?

By the time of the Commission meeting, plans for a re-enactment of the bombardment had been cut back to the merest token: the firing of a salute to the historic opening gun of the war. But the gunners of 1961 were unable to cope with a steady, heavy rain. A special correspondent of the Chicago *Tribune* reported: "The eight-inch fuse burned fitfully against the battering of the rain and fizzled out. Fort Sumter—1961 version—was safe."

The Fort Sumter fiasco has itself become history. What of the re-enactments in prospect?

Holly Springs should be a beauty. In the fall of 1862, Grant, then fairly embarked on the Vicksburg campaign, built up a huge supply depot at this Mississippi town on the Mississippi Central Railroad. The place was protected, inadequately, by a single Wisconsin regiment commanded by an officer who was both coward and dolt. Early on the morning of December 20, the Confederate Earl Van Dorn attacked with a force of 3,500 mounted men, found most of the defenders asleep, and captured the place without even a show of resistance.

Then the fun began. According to a contemporary Confederate account, published in the Richmond *Dispatch:*

The extensive buildings of the Mississippi Central depot . . . were filled with supplies of clothing and commissary stores. Outside of the depot the barrels of flour were estimated to be half a mile in length, and a hundred and fifty feet through, and fifteen feet high. Turpentine was thrown over this, and the whole amount destroyed. Uptown, the court-house, and public buildings, livery stables, and all other capacious establishments were filled, ceiling high, with medical and ordnance stores. These were all fired, and the explosion of one of the buildings, in which was stored one hundred barrels of powder, knocked down nearly all the houses on the south side of the square. Surely such a scene of devastation was never before presented to the eye of man.

If the script for the re-enactment is to be realistic, it will call for the explosion of 1,809,000 fixed cartridges, the destruction of 5,000 rifles and 2,000 revolvers, the burning of 100,000 uniforms and 1,000 bales of cotton.

Fortunately, dramatic dialogue does not need to be invented in this instance. Again we resort to the account already quoted:

The ladies rushed out from the houses, wild with joy, crying out: "There's some at the Fair Grounds, chase them, kill them, for God's sake!" One lady said that "the Federal commandant of the post is in my house; come and catch him;" and a search was instituted but without success, when the noble woman insisted that he was there, concealed; and finally, after much ado, the gallant Col. Murphy . . . was pulled out from under his bed, and presented himself in his nocturnal habiliments to his captors.

The provost-marshal was also taken, and addressing Gen. Van Dorn, said: "Well, General, you've got us fairly this time. I knowed it. I was in my bed with my wife when I heard the firing, and I at once said: 'Well, wife, it's no use closing our eyes or hiding under the clothes, we've gone up.' "

Obviously, there are dramatic possibilities, even to elements of bedroom farce, in a portrayal of the raid on Holly Springs.

But the engagement that I should really like to see is Brice's Cross Roads. In early June, 1864, a Federal force consisting of 4,800 infantry, 3,000 cavalry, and 18 guns, all commanded by General Samuel D. Sturgis, set out from Memphis to run down that pesky Confederate cavalryman Nathan Bedford Forrest and teach him a lesson. Learning of the Federal advance, Forrest, never backward, decided to give battle. About noon on June 10, he hit Sturgis' advance brigade at Brice's Cross Roads, in northwestern Mississippi. After several hours of hard fighting, the Federal flanks began to give way. What happened then has never been described more vividly than it was by John Merillees, a young lieutenant in Waterhouse's battery, Illinois Light Artillery. Merillees wrote:

> The order was issued to move the Artillery to the rear as fast as possible. . . . The supply train of over 200 Wagons, with nine days rations, had been, with astonishing carelessness, corraled within a quarter of a mile of the battlefield, and no effort made to get it to the rear, till the troops retreating filled the road, and it became impossible to remove it. Most of the mules were unhitched at the last moment and ridden off, but not a single wagon was brought away. The column now continued moving slowly forward, hard fighting going on in the rear, and the enemy shelling us vigorously, till darkness began to fall, when the firing gradually ceased.

The expedition pulled itself together, separated commands were reunited, and the retreat continued in relatively good order. About 9:00 o'clock in the evening the column came to a halt. Merillees rode ahead to see what the trouble was. His diary continues:

> The scene that met the eye was little less than appalling: the head of the column had reached the big swamp we crossed in the morning, and had commenced passing over, but no one being there to give orders, or no orders being attended to, a general rush of [gun] carriages had been made for the road which with the late rains was in

very bad order, and now it was nothing but a gulf of mud and water, the whole passage jammed with a mass of men, horses, wagons, ambulances and artillery plunging and floundering in the abyss, carriages dashing recklessly into each other, getting smashed up and turned over, the drivers yelling, lashing, swearing, and making night hideous, and getting the passage so hopelessly blockaded that it was impossible to get either one way or the other.

The awful bedlam continued until midnight. General Sturgis could not be found; the officers on the spot held a council and decided to destroy the artillery and ammunition, abandon all other supplies, and extricate the men. Before dawn the column was on the march. "The wounded begged hard to be taken along," Merillees recorded, "but that was impossible, and they were left in the ambulances with a sufficient supply of medicines."

Shortly after daybreak a detachment of Confederate cavalry fell on the retreating Federals but were stoutly resisted. A rear guard of Union cavalry dashed up, and the 59th U.S. Colored Infantry came in on the double, "with a coolness," Merillees wrote, "worthy of old troops. The indifference of the niggers to wounds was astonishing; numbers shot in the arms, hands, legs, their clothing soaked with blood, marching along with the rest, without a sign of pain."

Thus ended the Battle of Brice's Cross Roads. Can any re-enactment conceivably possible achieve the Civil War Centennial Commission's announced aim of making the truth clear?

I turn from re-enactments to some of the other centennial activities now in progress. We learn, through the Commission's official news sheet, that members of the Hagerstown, Maryland, Civil War Round Table are wearing uniforms of the Civil War period each summer week end and will continue to do so until 1962. "Daily newspapers," the notice adds, "recently reported that the sight of uniforms is drawing thousands of visitors to the parks in the Antietam battlefield area"—and, no doubt, to the motels, restaurants, and souvenir shops.

From the same source, the Commission's news letter, we learn that a member of the New Hampshire Civil War Commission is recording on tape "the sound of a Minie ball at 200 yards: the smack of its impact into pine board, the whine of its ricochet off water and off stone, and other sounds heard by the soldiers who fought a century ago." I wonder whether this sonic expert intends to include the sound of a .58 caliber soft lead bullet smacking into the human belly, or the sounds that came from a field hospital where surgeons, their bare arms dripping blood, amputated arms and legs without anaesthetics.

In May, 1960, the Commission's newsletter carried this titillating announcement: "The Civil War Centennial theme is to be applied, with the blessing of the National Commission, to the race track. From the Garden State Race Track Association comes announcement that it will devote two days of its season next month to this subject, and will continue to do so each year throughout the Centennial."

(Remember how the centennial was to bring about "a deeper understanding of the immense reserves of bravery, of sacrifice, and of idealism which lie in the American character"?)

Appropriately, the track chose the Memorial Day week end for its commemorative races, among them the Jersey Derby, first run in 1864. The entire track personnel wore Civil War uniforms and costumes. (Did the parimutuel clerks appear as guerrillas?) On hand for the Derby were Bally Ache, Venetian Way, Celtic Ash—and Karl S. Betts, who presented the cup to the owner of the winner. The crowd of 52,000 set a record.

The time has come to tell the story of William H. Tebbetts. I know him only through his letters, some of which I acquired for the Illinois State Historical Library about twenty years ago. In 1853 this young man, with his wife and child, left his native New Hampshire for what he hoped would be a better life in Illinois. In the next eight years he moved from town to town—La Salle, Peoria, Metamora, Sparta, Galesburg, Wataga—and engaged in teaching school, farming, and selling coal. No occupation worked out well. By

1861 it was obvious that Tebbetts had been successful only in procreation, having, by that time, increased the number of his children from one to five.

On December 5, 1861, Tebbetts wrote a letter to his parents from Camp Douglas, Chicago—the concentration point for Union volunteers from northern Illinois:

> You wanted to hear me state the reason why Albert, Edwin [two brothers-in-law] & I enlisted. Well I will tell you the sole reason why we enlisted was because our country needed our service. We could not bear the thought of seeing two thirds of the men in our town leaving their business and rushing to the battle field and to see them repeatedly whiped and we staying at home like cowards until those rebels tear down and destroy the best government that ever was; a government for which our forefathers fought bled and died; but I closed my school . . . and took my school boys and Albert & Edwin and went forth, gun in hand and our knapsacks strapped on our backs, saying that we will conquer or we will die.

Tebbetts's next letter, written from Camp Douglas on January 4, 1862, predicted that his regiment would soon leave for the front. On March 2 he wrote from Fort Donelson. He had been in the battles of Fort Henry and Fort Donelson, and had escaped with no more than a bruise from a spent bullet. The experience, however, had been awesome:

> I have seen trees a foot and a half through cut entirely off by the canon balls, and I have had balls strike the trees at full force not more than a foot from my head and I have had shells burst within a rod of me and throw the dirt all over me but it appears that the Lord has still more work for me to do. I enlisted to defend the rights of my country. I came here for the purpose of fighting. I expect to fight till the last armed foe expires.

One month later William H. Tebbetts, Private, Company K, 45th Illinois Infantry, was killed at Shiloh.

I turn again to the newsletter of the Civil War Centennial

Commission. The issue for May, 1960, quoted with approval a Prentice-Hall Management Letter of March 28, asserting that the centennial meant business and promotional opportunities for a wide range of retail and industrial firms. "Make plans now," the letter urged, "for new products and styles in clothing, furniture, home decoration, foods, and toys— based on the Civil War motif."

This theme was elaborated in an article entitled "Civil War Centennial: Business Merchandizes the Big Celebration," which appeared in *Business Week* for August 20, 1960. Here the prediction was made that the anniversary would occasion "the biggest outpouring of hobby money in history." Flagmakers were reporting that a substantial part of their sales was coming from Civil War flags and pennants. Tourism directed to Civil War battlefields had become of great importance to several Southern states. Clothing manufacturers were turning out thousands of blue and gray uniforms. One gun dealer in New Jersey had had 2,000 replica rifles made in Italy in what he feared was a wild speculation; he had repeated his order. Foremost Dairies, Inc., a southern firm, planned to concoct several "Civil War flavored" ice creams in the next four years. A swarm of companies, *Business Week* asserted, would turn out Civil War toys, stationery, games, men's accessories, buttons, and ash trays. And—again on the authority of *Business Week*—one state centennial commissioner was "trying to dissuade a clothing manufacturer from bringing out ladies' undergarments sporting the Confederate flag."

A recent article in *Newsweek* (March 27, 1961) adds evidence. Although the temptation to quote at length is strong, one summary paragraph will suffice:

> The centennial will be a bonanza for such specialized industries as diorama makers and "civic celebration management" firms [stagers of pageants]. The fireworks industry looks for a one-third increase in annual sales. Publishers are already issuing Civil War books by the shelf. Advertisers will find Civil War "tie-ins" for everything from frozen foods to jet planes. Record firms

will sell enough Civil War music to shatter the stillness at Appomattox. What with games and gimcracks, plastic cannon balls and model gunboats, Americans will probably spend more money on or because of the centennial than the $9 billion the North and South spent to fight the war itself.

Mr. Betts is said to have commented: "it will be a shot in the arm for the whole American economy."

Newsweek's story contains the interesting "intelligence"—a term that would have been used in 1861—that Foremost Dairies had given up its plan to produce Civil War flavored ice cream but would print battle scenes on its milk cartons. In the matter of the lingerie maker there was no report.

This is the place for the story of Day Elmore.

A week after the disastrous Federal defeat at Bull Run in July, 1861, the citizens of Geneva, Illinois, held a meeting for the purpose of raising a regiment from the Fox River valley. Among those who caught the war fever was a boy named Day Elmore, who had left his home in Trumansburg, New York, to work on the farm of relatives in Illinois. I do not know his age, but he was so young that he had to ask his father's permission to enlist. Permission granted, Day signed the roll as a drummer in Company H, 36th Illinois Infantry. The regiment served for several months in Missouri, and then was sent across the Mississippi to Kentucky. In the Battle of Perryville, October, 1862, it took heavy losses. It fought at Murfreesboro, or Stone's River, at the turn of the new year, going in with 600 men and ending the three bloody days with 200. It was in the line of battle at Chickamauga in September, 1863, where Day Elmore, no longer a drummer but a fighting man and a sergeant, was wounded in the chest. He recovered, and re-enlisted as a veteran. In February, 1864, his regiment was sent home on veterans' furlough. On the day the 36th Illinois reached Chicago, Day wrote to his father and mother. His letter, along with all the others he wrote to his parents, is in the collection of the Chicago Historical Society. I quote from it:

. . . We had a Grand time and a good Supper today at the expense of the Chicago ladies Bless them.

They took hold of our old tatterd flag and kissed it and sung Rally Round the flag. The col made a short speech with others. I was so overjoyed that my feelings had to come out and they did in a flood of tears. Pa if you could see that old torn flag and scarred yet you would not wonder that I love them. No Pa while the old and tryed 36 are in the field fighting for that flag and this Good old Union [never] will Day Elmore give up the contest if God spares my life. Today when I see the feeling the people had for us . . . and see thoes Ladies take hold of the old flag and weep while the col was talking I made up my mind I could stand anything for them even death its self if need be. . . . Pa look at this the day the thirty six signed there names to the new Rolls the *Ink* would *freese* in the pen before one man could write his name and would have to be brok out for the next to sign. When men do that do you think they inlist for fun? No they inlist becaus they love there country and the old torn and mangled flag and they were on less than quarter Rations at the time with out shelter only as they made them out of Rails.

The signature was a proud one: "Your veteran soldier son Day."

The 36th Illinois returned to the seat of war, and fought its way to Atlanta with Sherman. While there the terms of the three-year men who had not re-enlisted ran out. The occasion inspired Day to write to his parents.

Atlanta Ga Sept 23rd 1864

. . . Today we parted with the larger portion of our Regiment they having not reenlisted and now there remains but a small squad of Veterans we having been thined out on this last *Campaign* and as I look back *three years* ago when we started out *Twelve hundred* strong and ask my self where are they the answer is scatterd from the borders of Arkansaw to the heart of Georgia. Pea

Ridge Perryville Stone River Chickamauga Mission Ridge Dalton Resaca Altoona Mountain Dallas Adairsville Kenesaw Mountain Atlanta Jonesboro becides many other Plaices mark their last resting plaice. To day has seen the beginning of the end of the Gallant old 36th Ills. Inft. It makes me feel sad to think of the fallen braves! Of my old mess of twelve in number there remains but Dave [Hartman] and I. . . . Little did we think there would be so few of us left to still stand up for the Right and our Glorious old banner. . . .

After the capture of Atlanta and before Sherman began the great march through Georgia the 36th Illinois—now, proudly, the 36th Illinois Veteran Volunteer Infantry—was transferred to Schofield's Army of the Ohio which, with Thomas' Army of the Cumberland, had the job of holding Tennessee and taking care of the impetuous Confederate John Bell Hood, who had abandoned Georgia to Sherman. On November 30 Schofield and Hood clashed in the nasty battle of Franklin. There Day Elmore was hit again. Along with several wounded Confederates he was cared for by a kindly resident. A week after the battle one of the Confederates wrote the following letter:

Commanding Officer Co H, 36th Reg.

I am requested by D. Elmore of your company to tell you that at the battle of Franklin he was wounded and captured. He was wounded through the left lung and his arm is paralised from it. His wound is bleeding so profusely that he is suffering considerably. It is thought best not to stop the bleeding as it would bleed internaly. He is at the house of my kinsman Mr. Joseph Baugh and has every attention it is possible for us to bestow. Orderly Sarg David Hartman died in the hospital laying by me a day or two after the battle.

The last letter in the Day Elmore series was written on December 18 by Capt. Horace A. Chittenden, Co. H, 36th Illinois:

Mr. D Elmore

Dear Sir,

I have received the intelligence of the death of your son Day at Franklin Tenn. . . . . I wish to say that among all the brave men that I have seen march to battle I have never seen a braver, cooler man than my loved comrade Day Elmore and the prayer of my heart is that our Father in heaven, in removing him from us hath only dealt mercifully with him and taken him to that brighter world where the trials and turmoils the strivings and bickerings of the men of this world can never come and where he hath rest through the mediation of a blessed redeemer.

There are a few articles of clothing and some small mementoes belonging to him among my baggage and I will dispose of them as you may direct.

On the back of this letter Day Elmore's father wrote: "Capt Chitenden Decr 18th 64 Day is Dead."

Since there are still a considerable number of sensible people in the United States, the antics and commercialism of the Civil War centennial have not gone unnoticed. Increasingly, General Grant and Mr. Betts have urged that the centennial be considered a commemoration rather than a celebration. Mr. Betts, in particular, has been searching for deep and lasting values in the anniversary. Speaking in September, 1960, at the Kentucky State Fair, he asserted that the

Civil War was among the few conflicts which *gave* something to future generations. . . . Within its passions and fire there became welded providentially the most unified Nation on earth, the United States. We may eternally reflect upon this much: What was lost was lost by us all, and what was gained was a common gain. They were all good Americans who fought in the Civil War.

Were they, really? In view of Mr. Betts's pressing responsibilities, it would be unfair to expect him to keep up with the hundred or more Civil War books that are appearing each year. I could wish, however, that he had read *The War for the Union: War Becomes Revolution,* by Allan Nevins, whom many of us consider the greatest American historian currently practicing the craft. There Mr. Betts would have found two short paragraphs indicating that the North, at least, was not quite a unit in sacrifice and virtue. I quote the first:

> Bounty jumpers, substitute brokers, and corrupt doctors appeared in noisome swarms. Their activities in all the large cities became one of the chief scandals of the war. Agents tried to palm off cripples, old men, escaped lunatics, and dipsomaniacs as substitutes. . . . Substitutes by thousands pocketed their payments and bounties, deserted, and sold themselves over again.

And the second pargraph:

> Even the New York Chamber of Commerce admitted at the close of the conflict that the city had sold the government great numbers of pasteboard and shingle-stiffened shoes, and recalled the manufacturer who apologized for a boot whose sole dropped off after a half-hour march by saying that it was designed for cavalry use. The war on one side produced countless magnificent examples of heroism and'self-sacrifice; on the other, it made dishonesty common.

To show that chicanery was not confined to the North, I quote the comment of a Confederate officer on greed and corruption as he saw them manifested at Wilmington, North Carolina, the principal port for blockade runners:

> There were numbers of Confederate officers . . . whose sole business it seemed to be to lay in . . . stocks of groceries and dry-goods, and by speculating and shipping cotton from Wilmington and Charleston to lay by gold in case of an evil day. . . . Talk about Yankees worshiping the Almighty dollar! You should have seen the adoration paid the Golden Calf at Wilmington during the days of blockade-running.

I return to Mr. Betts's contention that the Civil War *gave* something to future generations. It did. Note this short excerpt from the diary of Emma LeConte, a sixteen-year-old girl who lived in Columbia, South Carolina. She wrote amid the ashes of the city, which Sherman's army had just burned:

> We have lost everything, but if all this—negroes, property—all could be given back a hundredfold I would not be willing to go back to them. I would rather endure any poverty than live . . . as one nation with the *Yankees*—that word in my mind is a synonym for all that is mean, despicable, and abhorrent.

And another excerpt from the diary of Kate Stone, living on an isolated plantation in Texas:

> We hear that Lincoln is dead. . . . All honor to J. Wilkes Booth, who has rid the world of a tyrant and made himself famous for generations. . . . It is a terrible tragedy, but what is war but one long tragedy? What torrents of blood Lincoln has caused to flow, and how Seward has aided him in his bloody work. I cannot be sorry for their fate. They deserve it.

To revert to Mr. Betts and his address at the Kentucky State Fair:

> In establishing the Civil War Centennial Commission the Congress did not call upon the American people to *celebrate* anything. Rather, we are all to *commemorate* the sacrifices of the men and women of 1861–1865 who gave of their best for their convictions and then, when the passions cooled, came together as one dynamic and ever-enduring family again. It is something we may all be enormously proud of. . . .

I wonder. I repeat that it is unfortunate that General Grant and Mr. Betts have not been able to keep up with the literature of the Civil War, and specifically, that they seem not to be familiar with a recent book by Philip Van Doren Stern, *An End to Valor*. In this volume Mr. Stern is bold enough to ask a basic question: "What was gained by this appalling sacrifice of battle-squandered wealth and human lives?" And to answer candidly:

> It would be pleasant to be able to say that much good was accomplished, that enormous benefits to the reunited nation were gained. It would be fitting and right if the price paid in human suffering could purchase an equivalent amount of human welfare. . . . Actually, the period that followed the Civil War was the most grotesquely corrupt in American history.

Mr. Stern elaborates:

> The bright colors of American life—the dark green of the forest age, the yellows and scarlets of Indian times, the clear ocean-blue of the clipper ship era, and the bloodstained red of all the wars—were mixed to make the dull sodden brown that results when pigments of different colors are carelessly slopped together. Out of this mixture came the brown age, the age of the brownstone front, in which venality was masked by a show of pious respectability. There was little protest; rich and poor alike reveled in the dark brown mud and manure that lay deep around the hog trough.

An exaggeration, doubtless, but close enough to the truth to be painful.

But that was eighty or ninety years ago. What of today? General Grant, in a Civil War Centennial Commission press release dated March 1, 1961, had one answer: that because of the war the United States had become "the symbol of freedom and individual rights for all the peoples of the world." A somewhat different answer has come from Little Rock, Montgomery, Tuskegee, New Orleans, Athens, Charleston—and Trumbull Park, Chicago—all scenes of bitter clashes between blacks and whites.

Kate Stone, the southern diarist, understood: "What is war but one long tragedy?"

The Civil War took more than 600,000 lives—the lives of men young and full of promise. How many other lives were shortened by illness contracted in service, how many struggled through the years bereft of arm or leg, can never be known. Who can measure the sorrow of parents, widows, orphans? The lowest estimate of the cost of the war is five billion dollars, a tremendous sum a hundred years ago. But this figure does not take into account property damage in the South—thousands of farm houses and barns destroyed, whole cities—Atlanta, Columbia, Richmond—devastated. And even if it did, who can translate costs in dollars into terms of human hardship? What did it mean to return to what had been a prosperous plantation to find only charred rubble and the fields in weeds? What of the feelings—what of the problems—of the man who owned twenty acres, a cabin, a mule, and a few pigs, to find only the twenty acres on his return?

We know what it meant: tragedy. Perhaps it had to be; perhaps—although I doubt it—it could have been avoided. But one tragedy of the Civil War need not have happened: the irresponsible, commercialized centennial celebration we are embarked upon.

After Mr. Angle's article was in page proof, Mr. Karl S. Betts was removed as executive director of the Centennial Commission. According to Mr. Frank E. Smith, M. C. from Mississippi (and an author and student of history), members of the commission felt that "there was 'too much emphasis on the circus aspects' of state and local re-enactments of Civil War events, and not enough emphasis on scholarly research and 'those aspects of the war which help create unity.'" General Grant shortly resigned as chairman of the Commission, for personal reasons. (The New York *Times*, September 13, 1961.)—Ed.

Historical Miniatures

In 1953 two editorial representatives of Rand McNally and Company asked me whether I would be interested in compiling and editing a volume of American historical documents. "No," I answered. "Why not?" "Because there are several good collections already available, and anyhow it would be a dull job. Get somebody else."

That ended that, but only for the time being. Late one night a couple weeks later—I always think best late at night—I had an idea. I reflected that most historical documents are dull, but the situations that gave rise to them were often exciting. So, instead of a brief introduction in small type for the Mayflower Compact, why not describe as vividly as possible the desperate situation the Pilgrims faced when they found themselves in a new land without any power to establish a government? Then, in type, emphasize the introduction and let the document follow. I tried several pieces and submitted them to my friends at Rand McNally. The idea found favor and the book *By These Words: Great Documents of American Liberty* resulted.

I include here six of the introductions, omitting the documents that followed.

From *By These Words* by Paul M. Angle. Copyright 1954 by Rand McNally & Company

The Pilgrims Decide
To Govern Themselves
1620

The tide was right, the wind fair. The departure of the ship the English Pilgrims hoped would take them to a permanent haven in the New World could not be delayed. For eleven years, unwelcome in their own land, they had lived among the friendly Dutch of Leiden. Now they were sailing from the nearby port of Delfshaven. Not all could go, so those who were to remain gathered on the deck to say farewell. Kneeling, their cheeks wet with tears, the Englishmen heard their pastor ask God's blessing. As they embraced each other, many for the last time, the stolid Hollanders who looked on in curiosity found their own eyes dim. But, in the words of William Bradford, one of their leaders, "they knew they were pilgrimes, and looked not much on those things, but lift up their eyes to the heavens, their dearest countrie, and quieted their spirits."

Thus began the journey that was to end off the coast of Cape Cod on a gray fall day in 1620. The Pilgrims had left Delfshaven in a small ship, the *Speedwell*. At Plymouth, England, where they took into their group a number of Londoners more concerned with finding fortune than the peace of God, the *Speedwell* was joined by the *Mayflower*, a three-masted, double-decked merchant ship of 180 tons. Soon after heading into the Atlantic, the *Speedwell* proved unseaworthy, and turned back. The larger ship continued alone.

The *Mayflower's* destination was Virginia, but when her master hove to, on the ninth day of November, off a bleak and sandy shore, he knew that he had made land hundreds of miles too far north. Although the season was far advanced, he pointed the ship's bow to the south. Along the shore, waves foamed in angry breakers, while at what should have been a safe distance, he found one treacherous shoal after another. The next day, with the consent of his passengers, he turned back. On the eleventh the *Mayflower* dropped anchor in what is now the harbor of Provincetown. New England, rather than Virginia, would be the home of the Pilgrim colony.

Before leaving the Old World the Pilgrim leaders had obtained a patent that gave them the power to establish their own government. The patent, however, had no standing outside the limits of Virginia. Some of the Londoners, aware of that fact, now boasted that when they went ashore, they would do as they pleased, or, as William Bradford put it, "they would use their own libertie, for none had power to command them." Knowing that only chaos and disaster could result from the lack of rules for the common good, the Pilgrim leaders determined that no one should leave the ship until some basis of government had been decided upon.

One can imagine the scene as they gathered in the cabin of the *Mayflower,* smoky and rank from the flickering wick of its fish-oil lamp. In the dim light sat William Brewster, spiritual leader of the Plymouth brethren; John Carver, soon to become the first governor of the colony; William Bradford, wise beyond his thirty–one years; Miles Standish the soldier, plump, sturdy, as short in temper as in stature; John Alden, the tall, blond, blue-eyed cooper—all sober, godly men, well aware that in this uninhabited land, thousands of miles from their mother country, they could rely on none but themselves. Many of them knew the covenants by which their congrega-tions—"independent" of the Church of England—were regulated. These they took as their model. The document they drew up we call the Mayflower Compact.

The compact, signed by forty–one of the ship's passengers, set up the first democracy in the New World and served as the sole basis of governmental authority until the Plymouth Colony was absorbed by the Massachusetts Bay Colony in 1691.

Peter Zenger Fights
For Freedom of the Press
1735

Appointed Governor of the Royal Province of New York in the summer of 1732, William Cosby lost no time in making himself unpopular. A man of limited intelligence, imperfect education, and no prudence whatever, he had more than his share of greed, pomposity, and bad temper. By a grasping effort to deprive his predecessor of his share of the rewards of the office, Cosby won the contempt of a large proportion of the inhabitants. Contempt changed to bitter antagonism when the Governor refused to grant lands to settlers unless he received a share himself, oppressed the Quakers, and arbitrarily dismissed the Chief Justice of the Supreme Court. Within a few months Cosby's only supporters were the provincial officers and a number of other favored colonists who profited by his patronage.

Yet the popular party—a large majority of New York's ten thousand inhabitants—had no way of expressing their discontent. The proprietor of the only newspaper—the *New York Weekly Gazette*—was also the public printer, and would admit no criticism of the Governor to his columns. The leaders of the opposition decided to establish a paper of their own. For a dozen years John Peter Zenger had been scraping a lean living from a small print shop; now he was induced to establish the *New York Weekly Journal.* Zenger, born in the Palatinate, was not too sure of English grammar and spelling, but his supporters supplied him with articles holding Cosby and the court party up to ridicule. New Yorkers read the *Journal,* sometimes in such numbers that extra editions had to be run off.

The Governor writhed. Twice he persuaded the Chief Justice to ask grand juries to indict Zenger for libel, but they refused. As a last resort the Governor's Council issued a warrant for Zenger's arrest—an act of doubtful legality—on the ground that he had published "seditious libels" which tended to raise "factions and tumults" among the people and to inflame their minds "with contempt of His Majesty's government." Failing to raise the excessive bail set by the court, Zenger remained in jail. While he was there, the Attorney General charged him by information (a method of instituting a criminal proceeding without an indictment) with having printed articles that were "false, scandalous, malicious, and seditious."

Zenger's attorneys, two prominent members of the popular party, began their defense by challenging the legality of the commissions of the two judges who composed the court. The judges retaliated by disbarring the attorneys, thus preventing them from representing Zenger at the trial. Having no confidence in the young lawyer whom the court had appointed to defend their client, Zenger's original lawyers quietly appealed to Andrew Hamilton of Philadelphia, reputed to be the ablest advocate in the colonies, to take the case. Hamilton accepted.

The judges, clad in black robes and heavy wigs, took their seats on the morning of August 4, 1735. The little courtroom was crowded to the limit, for the people of the province saw this case as the last stand against an arbitrary and oppressive administration. When Hamilton appeared, the members of the court party lost some of their aplomb. Although racked by gout and no longer young, his fine mind was vigorous as ever and his powers of persuasion known and feared.

As soon as the jury was chosen, the Attorney General opened the case by reading the information. Hamilton readily admitted that what Zenger had printed was libelous if false, but contended that the prosecution had to prove it to be false. The Attorney General, on the other hand, took the position that truth was no defense. Any statements, he asserted, that were "scandalous, seditious," and of a tendency "to disquiet the minds of the people" were libelous, even though true. Truth, in fact, made a libel the more malicious. This was the accepted law of England at the time, and the Chief Justice indicated plainly that he inclined to the prosecution's view of the case.

Hamilton's only hope was to convince the jury that this interpretation led inevitably to tyranny. His argument was lengthy but persuasive.

The jury deliberated for only a few minutes before it brought in a verdict of not guilty. "Upon which," Zenger himself wrote, "there were three huzzas in the hall." The next day he was discharged.

On the night of the trial the popular party toasted Hamilton at the Black Horse Tavern. When he left for Philadelphia the following morning, ships lying in the harbor honored him with salutes. A month later the Common Council voted him the freedom of the city, symbolized by a seal encased in a gold box purchased by public subscription.

After more than two centuries the freedom of the press has not been established beyond attack and dispute, but the gouty lawyer of Philadelphia still holds the honor of the first great victory over repression.

Free and Independent States
1776

When the delegates to the First Continental Congress left for their homes at the end of October, 1774, they agreed to meet again on May 10, 1775, if the colonies and Great Britain were still at odds. The winter passed with little friction, but in the spring the smoldering fire of revolt broke into flame. In mid–April the British military governor of Massachusetts heard that the colonists had collected a supply of muskets and gunpowder at Concord. On the evening of the eighteenth he ordered a detachment of regulars to march out from Boston and seize the supplies. And that was the night when Paul Revere, anxiously watching the belfry of the Old North Church, saw a single light—"One if by land, and two if by sea"—and leaped on his horse to warn the countryside that the British were marching.

A hurry of hoofs in a village street,
A shape in the moonlight, a bulk in the dark,
And beneath, from the pebbles, in passing, a spark
Struck out by a steed flying fearless and fleet:
That was all! And yet, through the gloom and the light,
The fate of a nation was riding that night. . . .

The next day, at Lexington and Concord, men and boys who had considered themselves loyal Englishmen died for what they believed to be their rights—and exacted a toll from His Majesty's redcoats far heavier than they themselves paid.

So the members of the Continental Congress met again—at Philadelphia, as they had planned, and on the tenth of May, 1775. Many had served in the first Congress, but there were new faces, too—John Hancock, the wealthiest merchant in Massachusetts, who would preside in place of Peyton Randolph, soon to die; Thomas Jefferson, only thirty-two, but already marked as a man of learning and literary skill; and above all the venerable and respected Doctor Franklin, finally convinced that the last hope of peaceful settlement had vanished. In the ears of the delegates rang the words of Patrick Henry, uttered when the news of Lexington reached Virginia:

"Gentlemen may cry 'peace, peace' but there is no peace. The war is actually begun! The next gale that sweeps from the north will bring to our ears the clash of resounding arms! Our brethren are already in the field! Why stand we here idle?"

And as they pondered this stirring challenge, the delegates could see, in their minds, Ethan Allen and his Green Mountain Boys crashing through the defenses of Fort Ticonderoga and accepting the surrender of that outpost in the name of the Congress of which they were members. A few weeks later George Washington rode off from Philadelphia to take command of the Continental Army that had besieged the British in Boston. It was ominous that he should be met on the way by couriers with news of Bunker Hill—a defeat which American heroism, and the heavy losses inflicted on the finest troops of Europe, made almost as sweet as victory.

The members of the Second Continental Congress met, in the main, as loyal Englishmen. But when King George, in the late summer of 1775, issued a proclamation calling the colonists rebels and warning all persons not to give them aid and comfort, public opinion began to change. On January 1, 1776, Washington, who had declared six months earlier that he would make every effort to restore peace and harmony with the mother country, raised the Continental flag in front of his headquarters at Cambridge; and a few weeks later he openly advocated independence. At the same time Thomas Paine's pamphlet, *Common Sense,* swept through edition after edition and converted thousands to the necessity of separation.

By May, 1776, a majority of the delegates to the Congress had come to favor independence. All that was needed was an impulse, and that was provided when a convention sitting in Virginia instructed her delegates to move a resolution declaring the colonies to be free and independent states. On June 7, Richard Henry Lee, chairman of the Virginia delegation to the Congress, made the motion. John Adams, in one of the proudest moments of his life, offered a quick second. Debate began, but three days later the question was postponed until July 1.

At the same time a committee consisting of Jefferson, Adams, Franklin, Roger Sherman, and Robert R. Livingston was appointed to draft a "declaration" in support of the resolution. Jefferson, steeped in the writings of John Locke, the English philosopher and political theorist, set himself to the task, working in the second–floor bedroom and parlor which he had rented for the duration of the Congress. After incorporating several suggestions offered by Adams and Franklin, he had the declaration in what he hoped would be its final form by the end of June.

On July 1, when the great debate was to take place, Congress listened first to the reading of a gloomy report from General Washington on the state of the Continental Army. Next came a more cheerful communication reporting that the Maryland convention had voted unanimously for independence. After that had been heard, Congress resolved itself into a committee of the whole to consider the resolution that Richard Henry Lee had offered three weeks earlier. For a few minutes silence prevailed, for no one could escape the feeling that one of the most momentous decisions in the history of the world would soon be made. John Dickinson broke the spell by taking the floor to summarize, deferentially but with all the eloquence at his command, the arguments against independence. John Adams replied in a ringing speech, and the session ended.

The next day, July 2, Congress passed the Lee Resolution: "These United Colonies are, and of right ought to be, free and independent States." Then the declaration was taken up, argued over, and amended while Jefferson squirmed with the pain that all authors experience when outsiders tamper with their brain-children. By the late afternoon of July 4, the delegates were satisfied, and the Unanimous Declaration of the Thirteen United States of America, known to us as the Declaration of Independence, was adopted to justify to a curious and skeptical world the founding of a new nation.

Contrary to widespread belief, no one signed the Declaration on July 4. Two weeks passed before the Congress ordered it to be engrossed, and it was not until August 2 that the delegates who were present on that day signed their names. Others added their signatures from time to time for the next several months.

The Declaration, however, was published and circulated immediately after July 4. Throughout the colonies—now to be called states—it was received with acclamation. As militia officers read it to their companies, as heads of councils or assemblies proclaimed it to eager crowds, drums rattled, fifes shrilled, bells rang, and cannon boomed—always thirteen times—while rowdy patriots tore down tavern signs like the "Lion and Crown," burned King George in effigy, and drank endless toasts in celebration. The years of hardship, bloodshed, and dissension were yet to come.

John Brown Pleads
for the Downtrodden
1859

In the courtroom at Charlestown, Virginia (now West Virginia), the judge asked the convicted man if he wished to make a statement before sentence was passed. John Brown, weak from wounds, rose painfully. His heavy beard could not conceal his pallor and his eyes glittered with feverish brightness, but his voice carried to every listener in the room, and to millions beyond its walls.

Behind him lay a career of failure, grim zeal for reform, and madness. Always an Abolitionist, he had finally come to consider himself God's chosen instrument to free the slaves. As a man in his fifties, and the father of many children, he made his decision: he would lead the blacks in a revolt against their masters that would put an end to slavery in one bloody spasm. Meanwhile, he would strike such blows as he could against the system. In Kansas, only three years earlier, he and his sons had murdered proslavery settlers in cold blood. A year ago he had raided plantations in Missouri, carried off slaves, and escaped with them to Canada. He had returned to the United States with a price upon his head, yet no one molested him while he planned the stroke that was to lead to the Charlestown courtroom.

On the evening of October 16, 1859, Brown and seventeen followers swung down a lonely road to Harpers Ferry, the hill-shadowed village that stands at the junction of the Shenandoah and the Potomac. With a rush the little band assaulted and captured the United States armory and arsenal. While they waited in vain for the slaves of the countryside to rise and join them, the alarm spread. Volunteers and militia companies mustered, regulars and marines were ordered to the scene. Brown chose to make his stand in the engine house. Under the fire of the troops his men lost heavily; it was his fate to see two of his sons die in agony. On the early morning of the eighteenth the officer commanding the attacking force, a regular army brevet-colonel named Robert E. Lee, ordered an assault. It succeeded. Brown, wounded, was one of five prisoners. Two of his band escaped, ten lay dead or dying.

John Brown was indicted for murder, treason to the Commonwealth of Virginia, and conspiracy with Negroes to produce insurrection. After a trial marked by scrupulous fairness, a jury found him guilty of all three charges. As he rose to hear sentence pronounced on the morning of November 2, he knew that he faced death, yet he stood unafraid and unrepentant. And out of his warped mind came a plea for the oppressed of his country that still rings with the aspirations of humanity.

On December 2, 1859, John Brown died at the end of a hangman's rope. Yet the great marching song of the Civil War is evidence that of few men could it be asked more pertinently: "O death, where is thy sting? O grave, where is thy victory?"

Lincoln Dooms Slavery
1863

On a hot Sunday in July, 1862, Abraham Lincoln set out to attend a funeral. Three men accompanied him—Gideon Welles, Secretary of the Navy, William H. Seward, Secretary of State, and Seward's son. On the way to the cemetery, some miles distant, the men talked. Suddenly they realized that the President was making a momentous announcement—he had concluded, he said, that a proclamation freeing the slaves was an absolute necessity if the Union were to be saved. The war had been going badly—McClellan had just been driven back from the outskirts of Richmond—and the Southern Confederacy appeared to be impregnable. The slaves, he believed, were a great element in its strength. As field hands, they helped to keep the enemy in food, and thousands served with the opposing armies as teamsters and laborers.

He had given much thought to the matter, Lincoln continued, but this was the first time he had spoken of it to anyone. What, he asked, did Welles and Seward think of the proposal? Both men replied that they were inclined to favor it, but asked for time to reflect before committing themselves.

A few weeks later, in a full Cabinet meeting, Lincoln informed his heads of departments that he had prepared a proclamation of emancipation, and that he wished to read it to them. After he finished, several made suggestions. Then Seward asked to be heard. He approved of the proclamation, but he questioned the wisdom of issuing it after a series of disastrous defeats. Too many people, he feared, would consider it as a desperate expedient of an exhausted government, as the "last shriek on the retreat."

"I suggest, sir," he said, "that you postpone its issue, until you can give it to the country supported by military success, instead of issuing it, as would be the case now, upon the greatest disasters of the war!"

Lincoln laid the document away.

On September 17, 1862, McClellan's Army of the Potomac and Lee's Army of Northern Virginia lunged at each other on the banks of Antietam Creek in northwestern Maryland. After a day of bloody but inconclusive fighting, Lee turned back to Virginia. The North claimed a victory.

Five days later Lincoln called the Cabinet together. Instead of proceeding to business, he reached for a book which Artemus Ward, the most popular humorist of the day, had just sent him—*High-handed Outrage at Utica*. With obvious relish the President read a chapter. Then his mood changed:

> Gentlemen, I have, as you are aware, thought a great deal about the relation of this war to slavery, and you all remember that, several weeks ago, I read to you an order I had prepared on this subject, which, on account of objections made by some of you, was not issued. Ever since then, my mind has been much occupied by this subject, and I have thought all along that the time for acting on it might very probably come. I think the time has come now. I wish it were a better time. . . .

> The action of the army against the rebels has not been quite what I should have best liked. But they have been driven out of Maryland, and Pennsylvania is no longer in danger of invasion. When the rebel army was at Frederick, I determined, as soon as it should be driven out of Maryland, to issue a proclamation of emancipation such as I thought most likely to be useful. I said nothing to anyone; but I made the promise to myself, and [he hesitated a little] to my Maker. The rebel army is now driven out, and I am going to fulfill that promise.

I have got you together to hear what I have written down. I do not wish your advice about the main matter—for that I have determined for myself. . . . If there is anything in the expressions I use, or in any other minor matter, which any one of you thinks had best be changed, I shall be glad to receive the suggestions. One other observation I will make. I know very well that many others might, in this matter, as in others, do better than I can; and if I were satisfied that the public confidence was more fully possessed by any one of them than by me, and knew of any constitutional way in which he could be put in my place, he should have it. . . . But though I believe that I have not so much of the confidence of the people as I had some time since, I do not know that, all things considered, any other person has more; and, however this may be, there is no way in which I can have any other man put where I am. I am here. I must do the best I can, and bear the responsibility of taking the course which I feel I ought to take.

That same day—September 22, 1862—Abraham Lincoln, as President of the United States and Commander–in–Chief of the Army and Navy, issued the proclamation which he had read to the Cabinet. The war, he promised, would be prosecuted in the future, as in the past, for the purpose of restoring the Union, and he gave notice that he would again urge upon the Congress a program of compensating the people of the loyal slave states who would voluntarily adopt measures of emancipation. But with the promise went a warning: On January 1, 1863, the slaves in all the states which were still in rebellion would be declared "then, thenceforward, and forever free," and the military and naval forces of the United States would enforce the edict.

The war continued, with the states of the Confederacy unmoved by Lincoln's threat.

On January 1, 1863, thousands crowded the White House for the annual public reception. For three hours Lincoln stood in line, greeting bemedaled dipomats, army officers in dress uniforms, and the rank and file of his fellow-countrymen. Late in the afternoon he slipped away to his office, accompanied only by a few officials and friends. The Proclamation of Emancipation lay before him. As he sat at his desk, he worked the fingers of his right hand, cramped from thousands of handclasps: he wanted no tremor to mar the signature he was about to write. Then he took the pen and without ceremony signed his name.

"That will do," he said to the group around him, and smiled with satisfaction.

Contrary to widespread belief, the Proclamation of Emancipation did not bring about the immediate end of human bondage in the United States. It left slavery untouched in Tennessee and in the border states which had remained loyal to the Union, while in those parts of the Confederacy to which it did apply, it could not be enforced. Lincoln himself looked upon it primarily as a military measure. Nevertheless, it stirred the enthusiasm of the opponents of slavery, gave a new direction to the war, and made the Thirteenth Amendment, which did free the slaves, inevitable.

Lee Says Farewell to a Brave Army 1865

For the first time in four years the guns were silent. Along the line of the Army of Northern Virginia gaunt veterans lounged beside stacked arms and unshotted cannon; cavalry horses, their ribs pitifully plain, munched the spring grass. It was good to know that there would be no more killing, but an army takes no pleasure in defeat. Still, when the commanding general came in sight, riding slowly to his own lines from the farmhouse where he had just signed articles of surrender, the troops instinctively shouted their welcome. Then, suddenly realizing that the end had come, they fell silent. Hats came off, and tears rolled down weather-beaten faces. Men in tattered uniforms pressed forward to take Lee's hand, or even to touch the white horse he had ridden through victory and defeat. Controlling himself, the General spoke a few words.

"Men, we have fought through the war together; I have done my best for you; my heart is too full to say more."

The next day he issued his last order.

In the Service of Clio

In this paper, delivered before the Chicago Literary Club ten years ago and published here for the first time, I expressed certain reflections on my somewhat unorthodox practice of the craft of history. In spite of my flippancy, the subject is one about which I feel deeply.

In giving this paper a title obscure, if not precious, I consider that I have paid all necessary deference to Literary Club tradition. I shall not, therefore, follow that convention which would require me in referring to a person who is quite clearly myself, to resort to such locutions as the neophyte, the historian, or perhaps in this context, the hypocrite. Instead, at whatever risk of immodesty, I am going to be "I."

I entered the service of Clio, the Muse of History—which is to say that I got a job—thirty-eight years ago. My employer was an organization in Springfield, Illinois, called the Lincoln Centennial Association, which consisted of the usual officers, trustees, and $10,000—but only the president and the $10,000 counted. It had been organized in 1909 for the sole purpose of celebrating the one-hundredth anniversary of Lincoln's birth, and the success of its effort was proved by the fact that stories of the centennial banquet which the newspapers had refrained from printing at the time were still in circulation. For several years the Association attempted, but only halfheartedly—no cocktails, no wine—to repeat its initial success. Naturally, it failed, and finally quit trying.

Now, in 1925, it was being revived, but with a different purpose. World War I had brought a quickened interest in the life of Lincoln. A small group of Springfield residents saw a responsibility. Quite a few people who had once known their greatest citizen were still living: they should be interviewed, their recollections recorded. No one had ever systematically scanned the local newspaper files, fortunately preserved, of the Lincoln period, nor had anyone made a careful search of the records of the courts in which Lincoln had practiced. All this the Association undertook to do, and I was the person chosen to do it.

My qualifications, as I assess them now, left much to be desired. After graduating from college three years earlier I took a fling at the life insurance business. Then my mind turned to the teaching of history, in which I had majored in college. I had no passionate interest in the subject, and no impelling desire to be a college teacher, but it seemed to promise an easier life than selling insurance and, if my brief experience in that occupation proved anything, one that would be equally remunerative. (I've never made a better guess.) So I managed a year of graduate work, and then spent a year selling textbooks to pay for it.

I suppose it was the year of graduate work that led to my employment. The president of the Association could not have known that during that year I had read as little history as possible and had spent most of my time in reading English and American classics which I knew only by title. (Unless graduate schools have changed radically since my time, I would recommend the same procedure to every unfortunate who falls into their snare.)

As matters turned out, my ignorance made little difference. The Association, I had been informed, intended to transform itself into a small but very serious historical organization in the pattern, someone intimated, of the Massachusetts Historical Society. But somehow I found myself spending most of my time, in the first two or three summers, herding visiting school children to the Lincoln home and the Lincoln Tomb—an occupation of a kind in which I doubt that the secretary of the Massachusetts Historical Society has ever engaged. With the school children were interspersed distinguished visitors, lured to the city to speak before a cultural institution known as the Midday Luncheon Club. The very important personages were compelled to take the tour, and I found some consolation in the fact that by and large they were more bored by it than I was. Then there were memberships to be obtained. That initial $10,000 was melting away—not, I may say, because of any large drafts being made on it by reason of my salary—but nevertheless it was melting. Now, the whole apparatus of membership entails considerable correspondence and clerical work. Since, in the beginning at least, I was my own secretary, you can see that I had little time for original research in the life of Abraham Lincoln.

Then there was the annual Lincoln Banquet, revived along with the Association itself. All arrangements fell upon me. They would not have been onerous except for the fact that the good members were allowed to make up their own tables. Each person reserving a table was supposed to fill it, but rarely did. But let the secretary try to fill a couple vacant places for some of the strays he invariably had on his hands, and the fur would fly. I could not escape the conclusion that half of the people of Springfield wanted nothing to do with the other half. This problem was difficult enough, yet it shrank in significance when compared with the sudden epidemic of deafness which invariably struck the city a few days before February 12. As soon as table assignments were released it would suddenly appear that practically everyone seated back of the second row of tables was hard of hearing, and would simply have to be placed closer to the speaker. And quite often, personal influence and human frailty being what they are, the handicapped *were* seated closer.

Another Lincoln's birthday responsibility falling upon the secretary was the entertainment of a number of out–of–town members who made the pilgrimage annually. The group was led by a wonderful old lawyer and former judge who had two gods: Abraham Lincoln and his own belly. Abraham Lincoln took care of himself on February 12, but on February 11 it was the duty—or pleasure, I never could quite decide which—of Mrs. Angle and me to help the judge and his companions serve his other deity.

The basic ingredients for the dinner were assembled in

accordance with detailed instructions, conveyed in advance. Whatever else was necessary, including a gallon jug of Bourbon whiskey, would arrive with the group in the early afternoon. The judge would immediately put on his apron and pitch in in the kitchen, always finishing in time for a couple of rounds of old-fashioned cocktails, which he insisted on making himself in huge glasses which he had transported two hundred miles. I can still see him with the jug between his knees, and hear him exclaim in his high-pitched voice, after the liquor had begun to take hold: "God damn it! Ain't we having a good time!"

The pre-Lincoln's birthday dinners reached their climax with the baked oysters. Arrangements for this very special occasion began about the first of February when the judge informed us that he had ordered a half-barrel of oysters to be sent from Baltimore to our house. Detailed instructions followed by telephone almost every night. I was to find a couple of roustabouts to scrub the oysters, Mrs. Angle was to employ two waitresses, he would bring bibs, trays, ramekins, and everything else. When the great day came, all went without a hitch until the first round of oysters had been consumed. In all the planning no one had thought about disposing of the shells. The waitresses, rising to the occasion, found two wash buckets, and the rest of the elegant meal, an experience for a gourmet, was punctuated by the steady plunk of heavy shells into galvanized iron.

The visitation of the judge's contingent concluded with a final function—a gathering of the group and a few local people in his hotel suite after the annual banquet. One of these, in its way, was as noteworthy as the baked oyster dinner. This was the occasion on which "Just David" decided to pray for the sinners. "Just David" was a Methodist minister whose intellectual calibre and naiveté were indicated by his selection of the title of Gene Stratton Porter's saccharine novel as his familiar name. On this evening "Just David" appeared at the postprandial session. The jug had been out, of course, but our ministerial friend gave no visible or vocal sign of disapproval. After twenty minutes, however, he announced that he would have to leave, and would those

who were there do him a great favor? Would they kneel,
and permit him to say a prayer? The difficulty was that
everyone had a highball in his hand, and all were caught
off base as far as tables were concerned. All, including the
judge with his 225 pounds, knelt, each man holding his
drink and trying his best to keep from spilling it while "Just
David" spoke his touching plea for the mercy of the Almighty.

After seven years of such service in Clio's behalf I was
asked to take charge of the Illinois State Historical Library.
It seemed to me to be a very good idea. The Depression
was approaching its nadir, and I concluded that the State
of Illinois was far more likely to survive the debacle than
the Lincoln Centennial Association. In short, I ran for cover.
Although I have never regretted the decision, my prognosis
was wrong. The State of Illinois cut salaries and missed a
couple of payrolls; the Lincoln Centennial Association sailed
through nicely. The experience led me to formulate a rule
of action for times of economic disaster. Abandon the essential industries. Steel mills and automobile factories shut
down, utilities lay off men by the hundreds, banks close.
But historical societies and art museums and colleges and
universities somehow keep going.

And so I became a servant not only of Clio, but also of
the state. I soon discovered that I needed to acquire a new
set of skills. The fact that I had no experience in running
a library turned out to be of no more consequence than
my lack of historical competence in my first position. I had
to learn about politics, and learn fast.

Theoretically, the three trustees of the State Historical
Library were responsible for securing an adequate appropriation from the state legislature. In practice, the job fell on
me. It turned out to be easy. One found out who really
ran the show—usually no more than half a dozen men—one
became acquainted, and the job was done. So far in this
paper I have mentioned no names, but at this point I am
going to shed anonymity and state that two of the library's
staunchest supporters in my time were Richard J. Daley and
Abraham Lincoln Marovitz, both members of the Illinois
State Senate.

I had another supporter whose name I cannot reveal, but whose case illustrated a point. The administration was Democratic; my friend was a Republican. But every administration, whether Democratic or Republican, takes out insurance by buying a few members of the opposing party whose votes may be needed for the passage of two or three crucial bills. The price is modest—a few jobs, an occasional favor for the legislator's district. My friend—an Episcopal vestryman, by the way—was a bought Republican, yet he had a sincere interest in history, and would go down the line for the Historical Library. My point, if you haven't already perceived it, is that even rascals are likely to have some merits.

Jobs, rather than appropriations, made knowledge of the art of political maneuver imperative. The State Historical Library was supposed to be out of bounds as far as the dispensers of patronage were concerned, but this was a distinction of which the patronage men were unaware. So every now and then someone would appear with a notice to the effect that he (or she) had just been appointed cataloger or assistant reference librarian. Inquiry usually disclosed the fact that the appointee had even fewer qualifications for the position than the librarian had for his. In a situation of this kind two avenues of appeal confront the administrator. He can berate the patronage office and claim exemption from political influence—in which case he is likely to be told to hire the guy or else. Or he can maneuver. Maneuvering, I quickly discovered, meant first, stalling, and second, visiting the bar of the Leland Hotel for several consecutive days. Sooner or later a party wheelhorse would appear, whereupon some such colloquy as this would ensue:

"Jiggs, two or three days ago they sent me over a guy for an assistant librarian who couldn't be the assistant librarian of a fire house. What am I going to do about him?"

"Well, you know how it is, Paul. We've got to find jobs for some of these characters, even if they aren't any good."

"Sure, I know, but why pick on me?"

"OK, tell him to go back to the office, and we'll find something else for him."

And then I would buy a drink. The problem had been solved.

I soon learned that at least half of these notices of appointment weren't—and I suspect still aren't—serious. The job hunter gets his appointment (on paper), the department head turns him down, and he returns to the patronage office. There he is told: "Look, that guy is solid with the governor. We can't fire him, although by God! we'd like to! Sorry, but we've done all we can for you."

It was not always possible to keep out of politics completely. I remember the inauguration of the WPA Federal Writers' Project. In the beginning, the governors were given the opportunity of nominating supervisors. For some reason or other, now forgotten, my signature was required. I was caught, on a Saturday afternoon, and summoned to the governor's mansion. I soon discovered that the persons I was recommending had no qualifications other than party loyalty, and I was indiscreet enough to make some comment to that effect. "You talk as if all politicians are crooks," the governor snapped. I apologized as well as I could and scribbled for five minutes in silence. Then the governor spoke again. "You're damned near right." That was Henry Horner.

Then there was the campaign of 1936. I was drafted to write thirteen three-minute radio scripts portraying dramatically the achievements of the administration. I could have refused at no immediate peril, but I would have had rough going the next time the library's appropriation came up. On the other hand, if I accepted, and the Republicans moved in, I would have had an even rougher time. The rules are clear and fair: one cannot engage in political activity and then claim exemption from political pressures. But in 1936 it didn't look as if the Republicans would ever return to power, so I wrote the scripts.

They were awful. I remember only one with any degree of clarity. It dealt with the efforts of the State Department of Health to combat an epidemic of trachoma in southern Illinois. The Department set up clinics and undoubtedly alleviated or cured the disease in many cases. You can imagine the opportunity this offered: the poor mother on relief—remember, the Democrats were administering relief—taking Geraldine to the kindly nurse at the clinic and bringing her home, after the fourth or fifth visit, cured. Why shouldn't the mother have exclaimed, in a voice tremulous with emotion: "God bless Henry Horner!" Not even the publicity men of the Democratic State Committee had such a low opinion of the electorate as to require that the obvious conclusion, "And vote Democratic!" be appended. I listened to one broadcast. I couldn't have stuck with that one to the end if it had lasted more than three minutes.

One of my strangest ventures in the service of Clio, and one of the happiest, was the purchase of the papers of Major General John A. McClernand. McClernand, a fiery Illinois Democrat, sided with the Union at the outbreak of the Civil War, and undoubtedly influenced many others of his political faith to remain loyal. Impelled by dreams of military glory, he sought and obtained a brigadier-general's commission, and later was promoted to major general. At times, in the West, he fought well, but Grant finally became disgusted with his egotism and insubordination, and relieved him of command two weeks before the fall of Vicksburg.

McClernand's papers, nevertheless, were valuable. They contained hundreds of letters to and from the leading military and political figures of the time, and his headquarters files were complete. I wanted them.

The collection belonged to a grandson, whom I shall call, quite accurately, the major. Chronically in financial straits, the major was willing to sell, but he wanted a price. By some evil chance he had found the publication *American Book Prices Current,* in which the prices of all books and manuscripts sold at auction each year are recorded. There he had discovered that occasional Grant letters had brought as much as $75, letters of W. T. Sherman now and then brought $50, Halleck might be worth $25. The major had 100 Grant's, which meant $7,500; 100 Sherman's, or $5,000; and 50 Halleck's, or $750. Therefore the letters of these three men added up to $13,250, and of course they were only a small segment of the total.

I tried to explain that *Book Prices Current* was a very fallible guide: that while one Grant letter might be worth $100 another would bring no more than $15—these were the prices of thirty years ago—and besides, if one threw a hundred in one lot on the market he would break it. In vain. The major remained convinced that the collection was worth at least $25,000. I knew it wasn't worth anything approaching that sum, and even if it had been, I was powerless: the library didn't have the money.

One morning, without explanation, the major appeared at my office. He would take $5,000 for the McClernand papers. But there was a condition: he must have the money that same day. I accepted the price immediately—it was more than reasonable—but I could not agree to the condition. Could not. If I put on all kinds of pressure I could get a warrant in four or five days, but neither I nor anyone else could do any better. The major wouldn't budge. Today or never, he said, and I was pretty sure he meant it. I asked for a couple hours' grace. Perhaps someone in Springfield would be willing to buy the collection for cash, sell it to the state immediately, and wait two or three weeks for payment. I turned to my former employer, the president of the Lincoln Centennial Association, Springfield's leading citizen, and a man wholly devoted to history. He didn't have $5,000 but he thought he could find it for me, and he did. In half an hour I had a check.

But I dared not stop there. If a suspicious outsider got wind of this transaction he would be almost certain to conclude that it smacked of hanky-panky. Against that I had to protect my collaborators, if not myself. So I ran down the governor, explained my machinations, and obtained his approval. I returned to the major in triumph.

Only to find that he hadn't quite stayed put. I must be aware, he explained, that he knew this collection far better than anyone else—in fact, no one else knew anything about it. He could save the library a great deal of money if he were employed for a year to arrange and catalog the papers—in fact, he had decided not to sell unless he were given this promise. I was terrified at the prospect of failure, and equally terrified at the prospect of having an irascible, unpredictable old man on my hands for the next twelve months. "Six thousand instead of five," I said, "and we'll forget about your working here for a year?" He agreed. The major played a good game of poker. That afternoon I rode from his house to the State Historical Library seated on General McClernand's field chest, packed with letters and papers.

As I look back on this transaction I am compelled to admit that at today's prices the major wasn't too far wrong. He simply had to sell thirty years too soon. I am also compelled, in candor, to confess a certain personal pique. A few days after the sale was consummated I met an officer of one of the local banks. "You probably don't know," he said, "that right after you bought the McClernand Papers the major came in and took up a thousand dollar note we had long since written off. I think the bank owes you a case of whisky." In this delicate ethical situation I could only smile. And I never received even a fifth!

I never had any compunctions about the purchase of the McClernand Papers, unorthodox as it was. On the other hand, I still wish I had not engaged in a somewhat similar transaction.

There may be a few here tonight who knew a Chicago bookseller named Harry Dayton Sickles. Those who did know him do not need to be told that he was a drunkard, a liar, and a blackmailer. He also was able to come up now and then with desirable books and manuscripts. I knew Sickles only by reputation, and when he telephoned me one morning to say that he was displaying some very good items at one of the local hotels, my curiosity got the better of my caution and I decided to take a look. He had some Lincoln letters, nearly all forgeries (though good ones), a few desirable books, and—what really interested me—two broadsides published by William H. Herndon, Lincoln's law partner and biographer. These I knew to be rare if not unique, and worth, even then, much more than the $80 he wanted for them.

I saw all I needed to see in half an hour, and promised to come back that afternoon. When I returned, Sickles was

drunk. I told him that I only wanted the Herndon broadsides.
"Why not the Lincoln letters?" he asked.

"Because there are only two genuine letters in the lot,
and they don't amount to much. The others are forgeries."
Whereupon I was expertly and lengthily cursed for my
ignorance and presumption. A few minutes later Sickles drew
me aside. (By this time there were several people in the
room.)

"Say," he whispered, "you're the only person I ever saw
who could tell the difference between a genuine Lincoln
and a good forgery at a glance. I want you to go down
to St. Louis with me tomorrow just to vouch for this stuff
I've got. And I'll pay you $100 a day."

I finally got back to the Herndon broadsides.

"All right," Sickles said. "You can have them. Let's see
your money."

"But I don't have any money," I explained. "I'm buying
them for the state. You'll be paid within three weeks."

"Cash or no sale," he answered, and he meant it.

In the room was one of Springfield's gayer citizens.

"Tom," I said. "You got $80 cash?"

He had.

"Buy these two posters—he wouldn't have known what
broadsides were (in fact I'm not sure I do either)—and I'll
pay you a hundred for them." And so it was arranged.

Two weeks later Sickles telephoned me from Chicago to
demand that I send back immediately one of the genuine
Lincoln letters—and he emphasized the word "genuine"—
that I had stolen that night in his hotel room.

I still regret the Sickles transaction. Not because I paid
an extra $20 for two rarities—at today's prices they would
be a bargain at $500—but because I allowed myself to become
involved with a thoroughly evil man. It wasn't worth it; it
never is.

In 1945 I ceased to serve the Muse of History in Springfield
and transferred my activities to Chicago. On my second day
in my new position I was forcibly reminded that once again
I would have to acquire a new set of skills. Just before my
predecessor's death four months earlier he had employed

a new membership secretary. On various visits to Chicago in the interim I was informed that the woman was not only incompetent but also a troublemaker of the worst kind. The one interview I had with her convinced me that both allegations were true. On the morning of my first day she demanded an interview; I put her off until the next day. When she entered the office I made the mistake of closing my doors—I knew what I had to do, and I thought it should be done in private. I informed her that I was dismissing her. She had been an actress, and in the next hour she proved that she was a good one. I was subjected to tears, recrimination, self-recrimination—in short, the whole scale of emotional appeals. Finally I stood up to indicate that we were through. She smiled, glided forward, stretched out her arms, and in a voice which I can only describe as dulcet said, "You can't do this to me!" I saw it in a split second: an embrace, then screams and on the second day of my job I would have plenty of explaining to do. I sidestepped, ducked under one outstretched arm, and got a door open. And to this day I have never closed my office door, whether the visitor be man or woman.

The new skills, to be sure, called for more than quick footwork. In Springfield I had had to make up and follow budgets, but I soon learned that they were of the most rudimentary kind. They had nothing to do with income—that came from the state, appropriated for certain purposes: all one had to do was to hold the expenditures within the prescribed amounts. (That handy device, the deficiency appropriation, had not yet been invented, or if it had, it did not apply to the Illinois State Historical Library.) In my new position I had to learn to make sense out of an audit report. I had to become familiar with such abstruse subjects as the eighty percent coinsurance clause as it applies to fire insurance and extended coverage. I had to devise a pension plan. I had to plan membership campaigns and, concomitantly, publicity. That meant not only writing releases for the newspapers but also making innumerable appearances on radio and, later, television. I had to learn to make speeches to luncheon clubs and women's clubs and graduating classes—speeches with some touches of humor, without much serious content, and above all, not too long. And I struggled with personnel as I had never struggled with that difficult problem before. In the state service pay scales are inflexible: a typist knows for example, that if she is hired at $275 a month she cannot expect more than $325, and if she reaches that limit and is not satisfied, she looks for a job somewhere else. This was not the case, I discovered, in Chicago.

My real personnel problems, however, came at a different level. It was easy enough to buy an improved wheel chair for a prominent—and wealthy—patron, for one of the members of our board of trustees at that time was an orthopedic surgeon. The case of the Dodge club-coupe, however, was somewhat more difficult.

Early in 1947, when cars were harder to find than apartments, an old friend of mine in the automobile business let me have a Dodge club-coupe at the regular price and without extras. My wealthy patron saw it and decided that she must have one exactly like it, even to color, for her attendants. She made it abundantly clear that if I could get a car for myself I could jolly well get one for her. But where, and how? I would not impose upon my friend; in fact, I was reasonably sure that he could not duplicate the order. In distress I turned to a trustee who I thought might have the necessary connections. "This is serious, isn't it?" he remarked, and put the wheels in motion. Two weeks later I was able to inform the lady in question that if she would have her chauffeur call, with check, at a certain Dodge agency in Cincinnati he could pick up a dove-gray club-coupe.

Another phase of this particular personnel problem led to a spell of churchgoing on my part. I had been brought up, as we middle-westerners say, in the Presbyterian church, but when I went to college I decided that I had already listened to enough sermons to last me a lifetime. Suddenly, by invitations that amounted to commands, I found myself back again in church—not every week, but often enough to destroy any certain prospect of a Sunday morning's ease. The experience was mildly disturbing. I had reason to believe that my shepherd in righteousness had made, shall we say, the right kind of will, but I worried a little on those Sunday mornings. The minister always seemed to be directing his remarks to the occupants of our pew, and I knew that I was not his target. I took some consolation from the fact that at least I was in that pew while he was seventy-five feet away. As it turned out, I need not have been concerned.

Then there was the episode of the portrait gallery. Our museum curator had decided upon an exhibit of portraits of women painted by the famous Chicago artist, G. P. A. Healy. The exhibit and the manner of hanging it had been approved by the chairman of the museum committee—the portraits were to be on one level only, and with adequate space between them. Unfortunately, we had no sooner hung them than one of our influential patrons from outside the city appeared for her annual tour of inspection. This exhibit, she informed me, simply would not do. There was only one way to hang paintings, she insisted, and that was the way they were hung in the old European museums: floor to ceiling and frame to frame. I tried all the methods of persuasion known to Dale Carnegie, but the lady was adamant. It is an understatement to say that I was in an uncomfortable position. Both parties to the dispute had demonstrated their interest in the Society by substantial donations. I could not afford to offend either, yet I knew that I would offend one. It is all well enough to say that in a situation of this kind one should do what he believes to be right, but some estimate of future possibilities had better enter into the decision. The exhibit remained as we had installed it. That turned out to be the right guess.

More recently I have struggled with another kind of personnel problem. Several years ago a woman whom I shall call Miss Beck stepped into my office to say that she had just become a life member and would be spending considerable time in the library. She was middle-aged, intelligent, cultured, and I welcomed her.

Miss Beck soon began her almost daily visits. She also began engaging the library attendants—and me—in conversations from which escape was difficult. Those conversations soon revealed the fact that Miss Beck was a mental case, suffering from delusions of persecution—a fact confirmed by her own ready admission that she had recently been released from a mental hospital. She was and had been for a long time the victim of a conspiracy which varied in number from seventy-five to a hundred people. Most of the conspirators were prominent Chicagoans, including at least two who sit here tonight. At times I have been included in this select group; at other times I have been cleared.

To say that Miss Beck was a disruptive influence is to put it mildly. For years we all tried by evasion and often by sheer rudeness to keep her from talking to us. There were times, too, when she bothered other users of the library. But she was also funny, as people in her unfortunate condition so often are. One morning she asked an attendant for certain city directories. The young woman brought them, only to be informed snappishly that these were not at all what she had asked for. Robert Cromie, then editor of the Chicago Tribune Magazine of Books, was working nearby. Cromie, being a knight errant and disliking injustice, spoke up:

"Pardon me, lady, but you got exactly what you requested."

"Who are you?" Miss Beck snapped.

"I'm Robert Cromie, of the Chicago *Tribune*."

"What are you doing here?"

"Writing a book on the Chicago fire."

"Why don't you put it out and start minding your own business!"

And there were those frequent occasions when, after describing the latest machinations of the conspiracy, Miss Beck would ask oratorically:

"What do they think I am—crazy?"

Miss Beck should have been disposed of long before she was, but pity diluted our irritation. She had long since spent whatever money she had and had gone on relief. Sometimes she was thinly clad in cold weather, while all one summer she carried with her a heavy beaver coat, relic of better times, which I suppose she believed would be stolen if she left it in her room. It was obvious, too, that she was not getting enough to eat.

Finally it became evident that Miss Beck was literally

wearing out our files of Chicago city directories, telephone books, and newspapers. I had to tell her that while she could continue to use standard reference works, we would have to deny her access to these other materials. She left, and has not reappeared.

Just to show that all personnel problems are not in the feminine gender I could go into the case of the photographer, whom my associate and I have come to refer to as the New Orleans cyclone, but I have already dealt long enough with this phase of service to Clio.

* * *

Most historians are teachers in colleges and universities. In fact, I suspect that if they were to define the profession they would say that it consisted of those persons who possessed Ph.D.'s in history and made their living in the graves of Academe. Certainly this would be their definition of the professional historian, a term they delight in using.

Never having taught, not even a single hour, I have no first-hand knowledge of the way in which my orthodox colleagues spend their days or the subjects of their interest. I know, rather to my envy, that they are the frequent recipients of Fulbrights and Guggenheims and Harmsworth professorships, and that some of them have even come to occupy influential positions in government. But for their real concern with what they choose to call the "discipline" I must turn to the "literature."

That literature is so extensive that I can do no more than select a single, but I believe typical, example. I cite you a book entitled *Generalization in the Writing of History,* consisting of essays by twelve prominent historians—pardon me, professional historians—edited by Louis Gottschalk of the University of Chicago, published only a few weeks ago by the University of Chicago Press.* It seems that seven or eight years ago a good many historians were stirred by two bulletins

---

*Although published in 1963 this book is still a fair example of the historical approach which I deprecate.—P. M. A.

published by the Social Science Research Council. One of those bulletins "warned against the gratuitous assumptions and purposes that frequently underlie historical interpretations." The other "emphasized the potential aids to historical accuracy in the interrelations of history and the social sciences." The historians concluded that a third bulletin was needed: one "that should address itself primarily to the question whether the historian is at all competent from his own data and by his own methods to derive concepts that are neither so limited in scope as to be trivial nor so comprehensive as to be meaningless."

The proposed bulletin grew into *Generalization in the Writing of History*. In the Foreword to this volume we learn that historians can be divided into two groups: "descriptive historians," who write narrative, and "theoretical historians," who try to find in their subject "a basis for comparison, classification, interpretation, or generalization." (It's all right: historians like me are used to being ignored.) The theoretical historian, we are told, "needs to have some knowledge of psychology, esthetics, ethics, social statistics, or other disciplines that deal with the interrelations of human beings with social events and natural forces." (With "Just David," Harry Sickles, and Miss Beck in mind, I think equipment of this kind for even the alley variety of historian would be a very real help.)

I do not intend to offer a summary of *Generalization in the Writing of History:* I can do no more than cite a few passages which illustrate prevailing attitudes of the profession. Nothing seems better suited to this purpose that the last paragraph of Mr. Gottschalk's summation:

> Historians borrow ready-made generalizations, whether they know it or not. If they were to borrow them knowingly, they might be in a stronger intellectual position. They might then undertake to assay and refine their borrowed generalizations by whatever means—definition, qualification, reservation, conformity to known facts, logic, psychology, statistics, matched comparisons, genealogical endurance, or other

tests—might be most appropriate and, avoiding the more untried and unverifiable ones, make good use of those found valid. Perhaps in the process, if sufficiently motivated and properly trained, they might originate and advance some restricted, tentatively acceptable generalizations of their own. At the very least, the professional training of historians ought to include systematic instruction in how to deal with the otherwise stultifying ubiquity of generalization in the writing of history.

I'm afraid we live in two different worlds.

In conclusion I can only say to Clio, in the words of the somewhat promiscuous young woman in "Kiss Me Kate:"

I've always been true to you, darling, in my fashion,
I've always been true to you, darling, in my way.

And in my fashion, like her in hers, I've had a wonderful time.

Books as Factors in History

Some twenty years ago the Kingsport Press of Kingsport, Tennessee, looked for a way to emphasize the influence the book had had in American life. The Press commissioned Earl S. Miers and me to write thirty-six short essays, each devoted to a book which had at least moulded opinion decisively, and sometimes changed the course of events. The book need not have been a good book; in fact, some of the most influential books were very bad books. The essays appeared in *Publishers' Weekly* at monthly intervals during the years 1953 to 1956.

Mr. Miers and I selected the books we thought deserved notice. Then we chose those that appealed to each of us particularly, and independently wrote our initial drafts. That done, we conferred, but in our conferences we rarely changed more than a word or two in what the other had written. I believe, therefore, that I am justified in claiming the five essays that follow as my own work.

The project interested me because it was essentially an exercise in the technique of writing. What we had to say—and we did have to make a point—had to be said within the limits of a single page. My original drafts usually ran to five or six hundred words, and then had to be brought down to three hundred without losing anything essential. In most instances that was not easy.

From *Books: The Image of America* and *Doorways to American Culture*, by Paul M. Angle and Earle Schenck Miers, 1958, Kingsport Press, Inc., pp. 15, 20, 24, 31, 37

Mason L. Weems
1759–1825

A History of the Life and Death, *Virtues and Exploits of* General George Washington, *With Curious Anecdotes Equally Honourable to Himself and Exemplary to His Young Countrymen,* by Mason L. Weems, "Formerly Rector of Mount Vernon Parish"—better known as Parson Weems's *Washington*—is pure corn to the literate American of 1953. Compounded of piety, sentimentality, invention, bombast, didacticism, and old wives' tales—of every ingredient, in fact, except rigorous research—the book pictures one of the most rugged Americans of all time as a combination of Little Lord Fauntleroy and Sir Galahad. Who can ever forget the cherry tree incident, when young George, "with the sweet face of youth brightened with the inexpressible charm of all-conquering truth," confessed: "I can't tell a lie, Pa; you know I can't tell a lie, I did cut it with my hatchet"; only to have his enraptured sire respond: "Run to my arms, you dearest boy, run to my arms; glad am I, George, that you killed my tree; for you have paid me for it a thousand fold!"

But . . .

On the 21st of February, 1861, Abraham Lincoln, on his way to Washington to take the oath as President, stopped at Trenton to speak before the Senate of New Jersey. Touched by the proximity of fields on which armies of the Revolution had fought, he recalled, as a boy, the excitement of reading Weems, and saw himself again in the loft of a cabin, lost in the story of the Battle of Trenton, the crossing of the Delaware, the fight with the Hessians. Lincoln said: "I recollect thinking then, boy even though I was, that there must have been something more than common that those men struggled for."

Lincoln was only one of hundreds of thousands of young Americans nurtured by the fervent pages of Weems's book.

We of today, taking perhaps too seriously Doctor Johnson's jibe that patriotism is the last refuge of a scoundrel, can laugh at the Parson. Our forebears didn't.

Timothy Shay Arthur
1809–1885

When Simon Slade quits the honorable calling of miller and opens a tavern, Cedarville proceeds to go to pot. Young sons of good families become tipplers at first, then drunkards and gamblers. Fathers follow the same course, or break their hearts over the waywardness of their offspring. Wives and mothers writhe under the depravity of their menfolk until they end up in the lunatic asylum. Men die in barroom brawls. Trim homes slip into ruin, fortunes are swallowed by the rum pot or scattered on the gaming table. In the end Slade's own son bashes in his father's head with a whiskey bottle. The good citizens of Cedarville—mysteriously, a few remain uncorrupted—rise in righteous anger, shut the "Sickle and Sheaf," and resolve to close their town to the ravages of demon rum. Thereafter, one assumes, all is well.

It would be hard to imagine a worse novel than *Ten Nights in a Bar-Room*. In plot and character T. S. Arthur's lurid thriller makes a Graustarkian romance look like drab realism. The sentimentality of the book is vulgar, its sermonizing clumsy. Yet its sales ran second only to *Uncle Tom's Cabin*, and Sunday-school libraries pushed its popularity by circulating thousands of copies. A stage version, bejeweled with angelic Mary Morgan's plaintive plea, "Father, dear father, come home with me now," left few audiences dry-eyed.

Published in 1854, *Ten Nights in a Bar-Room* coincided with a wave of temperance agitation that had begun three years earlier, when Maine prohibited the sale of intoxicating liquors. The book led many a citizen to cast his vote for a similar law in his own state, and helped to form convictions that finally brought about the adoption of the Eighteenth Amendment.

Horatio Alger, Jr.

"If you'll try to be somebody," said Frank to Dick, "and grow up into a respectable member of society, you will. You may not become rich—it isn't everybody that becomes rich, you know—but you can obtain a good position, and be respected."

"I'll try," said Dick to Frank. "I needn't have been Ragged Dick so long if I hadn't spent my money in goin' to the theatre, and treatin' boys to oyster-stews, and bettin' money on cards, and such like."

So Dick the bootblack, a manly lad beneath his dirt and rags, opened a savings account and learned to read and write—all to the end that he might throw away his box and brush and become a clerk. Eventually he does—and one knows that his clerkship will lead straight to wealth and respectability.

Ragged Dick; or, Street Life in New York appeared in 1867. At once the book became a best-seller. In the next thirty years its author, the Reverend Horatio Alger, would repeat the same wishful story in *Struggling Upward; Strive and Succeed; Jed, the Poorhouse Boy,* and more than a hundred others. The hero might be a street urchin, the son of a village widow, or an orphan adrift in the West, but he was certain to be honest, industrious, and eventually triumphant, although the Reverend Mr. Alger often had to rely heavily on Lady Luck to bring off this dénouement. The public responded by buying almost two hundred thousand copies of the books in which poor boys rose to fortune.

For fortune was the invariable reward. To Alger, success meant wealth. One may doubt that he inspired a great many young Americans to emulate his heroes—after all, it was also the age of *Tom Sawyer* and *Peck's Bad Boy*—but there is more than coincidence in the acceptance by millions, old as well as young, of his own unquestioning belief in riches as life's highest goal.

Ida M. Tarbell

Forty years ago a certain small storekeeper kept a supply of kerosene for customers who still used oil lamps and stoves.

At frequent intervals a Standard Oil Company salesman would offer to supply the commodity at a price far below the market. The storekeeper refused to desert his independent refiner. He was no radical—quite the opposite—but his sense of fairness had been deeply affronted by the methods which the first great trust in the country had used in winning its commanding position. The merchant would have gone out of business rather than give those methods the tacit approval of even small patronage. Many shared his attitude. For an understanding of Standard Oil methods the country could thank Ida M. Tarbell. First in articles published in *McClure's Magazine,* then in her two-volume *History of the Standard Oil Company,* this energetic journalist gave wide currency to the findings of the courts and legislative commissions which had unmasked the maze of rebates, drawbacks, preferential freight rates, and forced combinations by which the early Standard Oil had achieved near-monopoly. It was a story, Miss Tarbell said, of the machinations of "a compact body of a few able, cold-blooded men . . . to whom anything was right that they could get, men knowing exactly what they wanted, men who loved the game they played because of the reward at the goal, and, above all, men who knew how to hold their tongues and wait." It was no less the story of one man, devoutly religious, of strong philanthropic bent, and superbly endowed with business acumen—John D. Rockefeller.

No corporation today could indulge in the practices which Miss Tarbell described. Legislation prevents; ethics, self-imposed, forbids. Both safeguards stem from a complex of causes. Among the first of these was the *History of the Standard Oil Company.*

Emily Post

"Manners," wrote Edmund Burke, "are of more importance than laws." Even though Burke exaggerated, manners have been a matter of concern to intelligent people for centuries. In 1745 Benjamin Franklin brought out a book of etiquette that ran through six editions in five years; at about the same time young George Washington was making his own copy of "Rules of Civility and Decent Behaviour." From their day to ours, arbiters of social usage have coached the public.

Emily Post's *Etiquette,* published in 1922, might have been merely another addition to an overcrowded shelf. But where her predecessors were often snobbish and concerned with the behavior of an imaginary social aristocracy, Emily Post dealt with common situations and real people. "Nothing," she said, "is less important than which fork you use." Proper behavior, therefore, was largely a matter of common sense and consideration for others; its rules were those which courteous, sensible people had agreed upon in order to live together in good will. The public accepted a guide written in this spirit so eagerly that the book has gone through seventy-nine printings in thirty-two years.

Successive editions of *Etiquette* reflect the changing standards of American life. The question, "May a young woman go alone to a man's apartment?" receives two pages of discussion in 1954; it was not even asked in earlier editions. "Etiquette in Business" considers the problems of the secretary who has to travel with her employer—a situation that confronted few if any women in 1922. "Telephone Courtesy," unmentioned in the first edition, now demands eight pages, while "Manners for Motorists" has grown from a short paragraph to a full chapter.

Emily Post has not only molded American manners; she also serves as a social historian.

A Radio Book Review

All his life Carl Haverlin, now of North Ridge, California, has been a bookman, not in a professional sense but as an ardent collector and an equally ardent reader. Some twenty years ago, as president of Broadcast Music, Inc., he undertook to use the nation's radio networks to arouse and promote interest in books and reading. To that end he asked reviewers all over the country to pick out and write about one book which they thought young people would be interested in reading. The reviews were then incorporated in scripts which were sent to all stations willing to use them at weekly intervals. The program, called "The Teen Age Book Parade," was on the air for more than a year.

I chose *John Brown's Body,* by Stephen Vincent Benet, which I consider one of the greatest books of our time.

Reader: "You're wasting your time in talking about *John Brown's Body.* That's a poem—a book-length poem—and *nobody* reads poetry unless they have to."

So they told me, the wise ones. And maybe they're right about poetry generally, but they're wrong about *John Brown's Body.* Hundreds of thousands have read it, and other hundreds of thousands will read it. And those who pass it up, without even a trial, simply because it is written in verse, will miss one of the real treats of modern American literature.

They will miss, first of all, a great story—the story of the American Civil War. I've read that story in a dozen different forms—in the dull pages of textbooks and in the profound studies of professors. I've read it in the recollections of generals—and in the homely letters of private soldiers to the wives and mothers they left behind. I've read it in the cold and technical comments of military experts, and in the lively pages of historical novelists. But I've never read it in a form so moving—yes, often so exciting—as Stephen Vincent Benet recorded it in *John Brown's Body*.

That is partly, I think, because Benet was a young man when he wrote this book, and he gave it the verve and vivacity of youth. He was born in 1898, the son and the grandson of regular army officers. Rejected for military service in the First World War, he went to Yale, and published two volumes of verse before he graduated. *John Brown's Body* came out in 1928, when its author was only thirty years of age. Fifteen years later, before he had reached the level of achievement of which he was capable, he died.

Now the remarkable thing about Benet was this: while most writers of his generation were washing their hands of the United States, and proclaiming the people of this country to be uncouth dollar-chasers, he was finding strength and inspiration in the history of the nation which they had spurned. Consequently, patriotism—not the shouting, flag-waving sort that confines itself to Decoration Day and the Fourth of July, but true, deep love of country—marks every page of his writing.

I think it was Benet's pride in the common people of this nation that led him to tell, in *John Brown's Body*, stories which the more formal historians forget or neglect. There is, for example, the story of Jack Ellyat, the boy from Connecticut who fought through Bull Run and the awful slaughter of Shiloh, who wasted away to skin and bones in Andersonville prison, and then, whole again, lay behind a low stone wall at Gettysburg saying to himself as he watched the gray wave roll forward: "This is it, this is it," until the bullets hit him like blunt fists and he had breath no more. There is the story of Clay Wingate, who rode with the Black Horse Troop in the Army of Northern Virginia for four years, unhurt by war until his leg was smashed on the day before Lee surrendered. There is Sally Dupré, daughter of a Southern belle and a scapegrace Frenchman, whose eyes were blind to Wingate's shattered leg when he stumbled back to a home in ashes . . . and Medora Vilas, who never lost faith in the boy from Connecticut, and in the end found her faith rewarded.

Of course *John Brown's Body* is also the story, as any account of the Civil War must be, of great battles—of Fort Sumter and Bull Run, of Shiloh and Fredericksburg, of Chancellorsville and Gettysburg and the Crater and Appomattox; and no less the story of great men—of Abraham Lincoln and Jefferson Davis, heads of the two rival governments; of Robert E. Lee and "Stonewall" Jackson, the idols of the Confederacy; of Meade and Grant and Sherman, who led the armies of the Union to their ultimate victory.

Through all these stories, and many others, runs that of the man from whom the book takes its title—old John Brown, the antislavery fanatic who was hanged for an insane attempt to free the slaves by insurrection . . . hanged for treason to the State of Virginia, but somehow freed by death to march through the years in step with a million men in blue—to walk, as Benet puts it, "in front of the armies . . . With his gun on his shoulder, his phantom-sons at heel, His eyes like misty coals." Let me urge you again not to be deterred by the fact that *John Brown's Body* is written in verse. Read a few pages, and you will discover that this poetry is no more difficult to understand than the simplest prose. You'll skim through the narrative without even realizing that there's rhythm to the lines, and sometimes rhyme. But not always, for every now and then you will come across a few lines so beautifully turned that you will say to yourself, "Why, this is a poem!" and be glad of it.

Across the Board: Reflections on Book Collecting

This paper, one of the annual Randolph G. Adams
Memorial Lectures, was read at the William L. Clements
Library, Ann Arbor, Michigan, on October 14, 1959.

Seventeen years ago a symposium on various aspects of
writing and publishing came out under the title, *Bookmaking
and Kindred Amenities.* The story goes that, not long after
the book appeared, a man wearing a checked suit, a large
diamond ring, and a horseshoe stickpin saw the volume in
the window of a small shop in Los Angeles, walked in, and
bought a copy without even looking inside the covers. When
the book was wrapped and the money in the cash register,
the clerk thought it safe to satisfy his curiosity. "May I ask,
sir," he said, "why you happen to be interested in this
particular book? It isn't exactly a best-seller." "Sonny," came
the reply, "I make my livin' off the ponies, and maybe dis
guy's got somethin' I ought to know about!"

I am sure that most of you will recognize the sport, or
business, or racket, from which my title is derived. If there
should be present some who do not, may I say that the
sport, or business, or racket, is horse racing, and that "across
the board" is that method of betting in which one picks
a horse to come in first, second, or third. The method is
not favored by a majority of true horse players for the reason
that the returns are likely to be much smaller than if one
bets to win—and guesses right. But the chances of collecting

From the *Michigan Alumnus Quarterly Review,* Vol. LXVI, No. 14, pp.
113–22

something are three times as good as when one plays only
to win, or place, or show.

I trust that this somewhat technical discourse will seem
less irrelevant as I proceed with my remarks.

Consider, first of all, rare books. I hope that what I intend
to say on this subject will not be misunderstood. I shall
raise certain questions about rare books and rare book
libraries, and I do not want you to think that I have accepted
your invitation only to criticize what has always been the
primary interest of the William L. Clements Library. I believe
I am as much interested as anyone can be in the acquisition
of a rare book and in the handling of it, and I am as thoroughly
convinced as any of you are of the value of libraries such
as this, the Morgan, the John Carter Brown, and the Huntington, to say nothing of the rare book collections of more
general institutions. Believing, as I do, that the book is the
most important means—by long odds the most important
means—of transmitting one generation's knowledge to all
succeeding generations, how could I hold otherwise?

I grant, without question, all that can be said in favor
of collecting and preserving rare books. I shall not argue
with the assertion that a first edition comes closer to the
author and his original intention than do later editions. I
am not immune to the sentimental or emotional appeal,
so well expressed by a recent writer in this statement; "There
is joy and pride in the possession of a valuable book, just
as there is satisfaction in owning a precious stone rather
than a synthetic substitute." I believe that the original *Bay
Psalm Book* enables an imaginative person to recall the
Massachusetts Bay Colony with far more fidelity than the
finest facsimile reprint can do, as I also believe that *The
Life of Black Hawk,* published in Cincinnati in 1833, gives
one a better insight into the Old Northwest of one hundred
and twenty-five years ago than does Milo M. Quaife's Lakeside
Press edition of 1916. To the postwar, pre-fire Chicago,
Jevne and Almini's *Chicago Illustrated* offers an incomparable
view, far more evocative in the thirteen original parts with
their covers than the bound volume assembled after 1871,
and in either state more representative of the time than

any later imprints, for one of which I am responsible.

I can quote, with entire approval, Miss Ellen Shaffer's summation:

> Rare books have an intangible worth apart from their value in the field of scholastic research. They give a sense of stability as we reflect that they have survived many vicissitudes and still exist to bring us at least a whisper of the immortality of man's accomplishments. They can recreate the past for us and thus are part of our cultural heritage. They may inspire us to achieve an important work, or they may simply add enjoyment to our lives—in itself no mean accomplishment.

But—and I emphasize the word—I do not think we do the rare book cause any service when we look down our noses at those who do not fully share our own enthusiasm. When we hear someone say that a microfilm copy will serve his purpose as well as the original rarity, we tend to consign that person to limbo. We might better admit that in a great many instances microfilm—much as I hate the stuff—*will* serve just as well as the original. Yet we might also take the opportunity to ask the person who makes this assertion how he thinks he could have obtained his microfilm copy if someone, or some institution, hadn't preserved the original.

I also believe that in rare books we are inclined to place far too much emphasis on first editions. Even the authors' later editions may be, and in fact often are, superior to the first. If a library could afford only one edition of George W. Kendall's *Narrative of the Texan Santa Fé Expedition,* it would do well to choose the seventh, which came out in 1856, rather than the first, which appeared in 1844. The third edition of Jonathan Carver's *Travels Through the Interior Parts of North America* is definitely superior to the first. The same can be said of Gilbert Imlay's *Topographical Description of the Western Territory.* As between the first and second editions of Gregg's *Commerce of the Prairies,* take the second, if for no other reason than that it has an index and glossary that are lacking in the first.

We would do well to admit, too, that very often modern

reprints are definitely superior, for scholarly purposes, to all early editions. I do not suppose that Juliette Kinzie's *Wau-Bun, the "Early Day" in the Northwest* qualifies as a rare book—scarce would be a more accurate classification—but it will serve as an example. When I have occasion to use that book, which is fairly often, I turn not to the first edition but to Milo M. Quaife's Lakeside Press edition of 1932, which has a critical introduction and footnotes that no serious reader can afford to miss. Frances Trollope's *Domestic Manners of the Americans* is commoner than *Wau-Bun* but it is another case in point. The first edition of the book somehow evokes "Porkopolis," as Cincinnati was then called, but one who wants to press out Mrs. Trollope's acidulous juice to the fullest measure would be well advised to use the Donald Smalley edition (Knopf). I hold, moreover, that when a travel narrative may be found in Reuben Gold Thwaites' *Early Western Travels,* he who uses the original edition instead of the text as found in Thwaites is little short of a plain fool.

Please note that I did not include *all* modern reprints in the above commendation. I have seen some almost incredible instances of careless transcription and incompetent editing in reprints—which is simply another argument for the careful preservation of the original rarity.

The propensity, among rare book collectors and librarians, which disturbs me most of all, is the concentration upon famous books. Why must so many of our brethren go to great lengths in their efforts to obtain certain well-publicized books and then stew in frustration when they fail?

I give you an example.

There are two libraries less than a mile apart. Library Number One has a copy of a very rare book, Thomas and Wild's *The Valley of the Mississippi,* published in nine parts at St. Louis in 1841–42. What is more, Library Number One's copy of this book is considered to be the best of the few that are known to exist. Library Number Two lacks the book. When a copy came up at auction a year or two ago, Library Number Two went to unusual lengths in an effort to buy it, but did not succeed. Library Number One's possession of a fine copy of *The Valley of the Mississippi* is widely known, yet in fifteen years the book has been consulted no oftener than half-a-dozen times, and then only for the comparison of bibliographical points. Why, I ask you, was Library Number Two so set on acquiring a copy? Why do so many libraries and collectors go after the McKenney and Hall Indian portfolio, the Lewis Portfolio, and the Maximilian, Prince of Wied? Why should almost everyone feel thwarted if he does not possess a copy of Collot's *Journey in North America,* with atlas, and preferably the English edition rather than the French? Why the incessant quest for the Cabeza de Vacas, the Champlains, the Lescarbots, the Hennepins, the John Smiths, the Winthrops, the Bradfords? Why the obsession with the extremely rare overland narratives when we already know, from readily accessible firsthand accounts, the full story of this tremendous mass migration?

I have no objection to this concentration of interest, except that I fear it distracts attention from many books equally rare, of comparable importance, but ignored because they have not received the collectors' and dealers' accolade. Permit me to offer a few examples.

In the library of the Chicago Historical Society are the first two directories of the very unusual city of Galena, Illinois. Both have the same title: *Galena Directory and Miners' Annual Register.* The first covers the years 1847–48 and was printed in Chicago; the second is dated 1848–49 and was printed in Galena. The two books are so rare that the man I consider to be the foremost Americana expert in the country had never seen either until we produced them from our collection.

In intrinsic importance, I should not put either on a plane with John Smith's *Generall Historie,* yet I should not hesitate to rank them with any overland narrative. The first of the two contains a description of Galena and a history of both the town and the lead-mine district, then the largest and most important in the country; the second has a long description of the lead mines and smelters of northwestern Illinois and southwestern Wisconsin. It is my candid opinion that one could find Riley Root's *Journal of Travels to Oregon—*

in fact I know the whereabouts of a dozen copies—or Oliver's *Guide to the New Gold Region of Western Kansas and Nebraska* more readily than one could find either of these two Galena directories. No one should expect to buy either Galena directory for peanuts, but he could be sure of acquiring them for a fraction of what the Riley Root or Oliver would cost him. And why? Because overland narratives are high fashion, town directories are not.

The Chicago Historical Society has a copy of John Brown's *Provisional Constitution and Ordinances for the People of the United States,* printed in 1857, who knows where. This was the framework for the interim government of the state which John Brown intended to establish when the slave insurrection he was already planning should have succeeded. On its significance I quote Allan Nevins, in *The Emergence of Lincoln:*

> Monomania has reached its climax. . . . In every feature the scheme is preposterous: the idea that slaves are ready for wholesale revolt; the idea that State and national forces can be resisted; the idea that a temporary new commonwealth can be created. Yet there is method in Brown's madness. The preamble of his constitution is a declaration of war which justifies the killing of slaveholders, the liberation of slaves, the confiscation of other property, and the ravaging of enemy lands. It does more than justify the fomenting of slave insurrections; it assumes that a universal and incessant slave insurrection is under way, and that only brute force is restraining it within bounds. Rejecting the American Constitution, Brown is establishing his own government and laws, under which he will be free to commit any act of belligerent violence. As he wages war against the slaveholders, the States, and the nation, his robberies will be called the confiscation of enemy property, his kidnappings will be termed the seizure of enemy hostages, and his murders will be denominated legitimate military operations.

Consider also the fact that if individuals may be charged with responsibility for bringing on the Civil War, John Brown must take as much of the blame as anyone else, not excluding Harriet Beecher Stowe. This pamphlet, therefore, cannot be relegated to an unimportant place in American historical literature.

I will not say that our copy of John Brown's *Provisional Constitution* is unique. I do know that it has no auction record, and that it is the only copy which Allan Nevins, a persistent searcher of libraries, found. Yet I am reasonably sure that if a copy did come on the market it would not bring a price approaching that which would be asked, and obtained, for a copy of the Constitution of the Confederate States of America, with a Confederate imprint, and this in spite of the fact that one can obtain the text of the Confederate Constitution from innumerable sources. The reason? Confederate imprints are fashionable.

A third and final example. The disloyal, or Copperhead, movement during the Civil War was personified by Clement L. Vallandigham, the Ohio politician who, in 1863, was convicted by a military commission of inciting to treason, banished to the Confederate lines, and later nominated for governor by the Peace Democrats of his state. The complete record of his trial was published at Cincinnati in 1863. Here is an important book without an auction record. I suspect that few copies exist, but I have an uneasy feeling that if one were to come on the market at the same time as Linforth's *Route from Liverpool to Great Salt Lake,* most rare book buyers would go for the Linforth instead of the Vallandigham trial record. Now the Linforth is a fine book, and one of my favorites, but my guess is that ten copies can be found in American libraries for every one copy which can be located of *The Trial of Hon. Clement L. Vallandigham.*

The collecting of maps follows the same pattern. In American maps, what are the great desiderata? I shall name three as examples: Thomas Hutchins' *New Map of the Western Parts of Virginia, Pennsylvania, Maryland and North Carolina,* London, 1778; Henry Popple's *Map of the British Empire in North America,* London, 1733; and John Filson's *Map of Kentucke,* Philadelphia, 1784. There are others, of course, yet no map collector, private or institutional, would consider his American map collection complete if it lacked any one of these three.

No collector, on the other hand, will lose much sleep because he does not possess John Melish's *Map of the United States with the Contiguous British and Spanish Possessions,* published at Philadelphia in 1816—a superb example of early nineteenth-century cartography; nor will he be greatly disturbed because he does not have D. B. Cooke & Company's *Great Western Railroad Guide,* Chicago, 1856, which shows all railroads then built or building in the northern states, from western Pennsylvania to eastern Iowa. Both maps are of more practical utility today than the three high spots I have mentioned, and I predict that the time will come, if it is not already here, when they will be harder to get.

If I have not yet made my position clear, let me state it summarily: I am criticizing only the collector who is guided solely by fashion, and I am pleading for more independence of judgment, more self-reliance, than is often exhibited.

This leads me to the field in which I think the rewards of independent judgment are largest: the field of books that are only scarce, not rare. Here I wish that more collectors would not be deterred by the fact that a book can be had for twenty–five or thirty dollars instead of five hundred.

What is a scarce book? Only last week I came across the following paragraph in the *Chicago Tribune* for September 8, 1909:

> For the increasing number of autoists who make the trip between Chicago and New York the *Photo Auto Guide,* just issued by Rand McNally & Co., would seem to be a necessary thing. It is a large book containing several hundred photographs, two to a page, showing the various turns in the route, and the intersecting cross roads, with arrows pointing the way to be taken. There are, for instance, 245 photographic representations of the turns and other directions on the road between this city and New York, and the landmarks are all identified so that there can be no mistake. The return landmarks

are also shown, and there are many outline maps for the direction of the motorists.

This *Photo Auto Guide* is not in the library of the Chicago Historical Society, nor does Rand McNally have it. I suspect that it is really a rare book rather than a scarce one, but if it came on the market I doubt that it would be priced at more than twenty-five dollars. (Unless, of course, the dealer who came up with a copy knew what I have just said about it.)

The *Photo Auto Guide* was once common and is now at least scarce. All of us who have been concerned with books for more than a few years have seen many instances of that transition. About thirty years ago I bought a copy of the *Memoirs of Gustave Koerner,* an important book that is still not as well known as it ought to be. Although published in 1909, the book was still in print when I bought it, and therefore the two substantial volumes cost me only six dollars. The book will cost you thirty-five dollars today, and be worth every penny of that sum. The eight volumes of Ray Stannard Baker's *Woodrow Wilson: Life and Letters* would have cost a total of thirty-nine dollars had they been purchased between 1927 and 1939, when they appeared. About two years ago I discovered that the book was not in the Chicago Historical Society's library. In my innocence I thought that it would be a simple matter to pick up a copy. The dealer to whom I turned laughed at me. We were not successful until last month, and then we had to be satisfied with an ex-library set, in only fair condition, and for it we paid materially more than the original published price.

I do not believe that either the Koerner or the Woodrow Wilson will ever be truly rare—there are too many copies in print. There are certain categories of scarce books, however, which I confidently expect to move into the rare classification. One such consists of the accounts of travelers in the United States published during the second half of the nineteenth century.

When I first became concerned with libraries, about twenty-five years ago, nearly everyone looked down his nose at a traveler's account printed later than 1850 unless it happened to be an overland narrative. Even overlands, to be considered desirable, couldn't be much later than that date. A five-dollar bill would have bought nearly anything after 1850 that a dealer had in stock. Now? I quote from two or three catalogs which have recently come into my hands:

Basterot, *De Quebec à Lima: Journal d'un Voyage dans les deux Amériques en 1858 et en 1859,* Paris, 1860. $25.

Bates, *Notes of a Tour in Mexico and California,* New York, 1887. $35.

Ferri-Pisani, *Lettres sur les Etats-Unis D'Amérique,* Paris, 1862. $20.

Horace Greeley, *Overland Journey, from New York to San Francisco,* New York, 1860. $30.

Downie, *Hunting for Gold, Personal Experiences in the Early Days on the Pacific Coast,* San Francisco, 1893. $35.

Here, I believe, is a fine field for the collector. Instead of regretting our failure to act earlier, we'd better plunge in before these books become even scarcer and higher-priced. Others have come to the same conclusion. The Basterot book was listed in the catalog of a Chicago dealer. The catalog came in the mail on a Monday morning. There are certain catalogs which the Society's librarian examines immediately; this was one of them. In a few minutes she telephoned an order. Sorry. Already sold.

Mention of catalogs leads me to another category of scarce books—catalogs. Not book dealers' catalogs but the catalogs of merchants and manufacturers, and especially those with good illustrations. Time was when only the early catalogs of Montgomery Ward and Sears Roebuck were sought for, but times have changed. A short time ago we paid sixty-five dollars for a small catalog of the Knickerbocker Ice Company, Philadelphia, 1878, offering ice wagons and the tools then used in the ice business. The dealer from whom we bought it informed us that ours was only the first of several orders, and that one librarian was quite disturbed because the item had been listed; it should have been offered to him privately. I admit that this is a specialized field. It happens to be one of very practical value to the Chicago Historical Society because our library is extensively used by advertising copy writers and by people working in the history of businesses. Many libraries would not have a similar need. But if one does have the need, now is the time to acquire. The supply will never be larger nor the demand smaller, and prices can go only one way—up.

The Civil War offers a fine opportunity to the collector or librarian who can be tempted by scarce books rather than rare ones. About twenty years ago the library with which I was then associated became the recipient of a substantial Civil War collection. By orthodox standards the collection was good—it contained nearly all the "important" books: the biographies and autobiographies of the leading generals, the standard histories of various campaigns. What it lacked was the unimportant books: the regimental histories, the personal narratives of soldiers who never wore the star of a brigadier. The donor of the collection had established a fund for further purchases, so I set out to add the kind of books which I believed to be desirable. Some of my associates were dubious about the purchase of such books as Leander Stillwell's *The Story of a Common Soldier or Army Life in the Civil War,* published at Erie, Kansas, in 1917, or S. H. M. Byers' *With Fire and Sword,* New York, 1911, and looked with misgivings upon my eagerness to buy books like Rufus R. Dawes' *Service with the Sixth Wisconsin Volunteers,* the *History of Sauk County Riflemen, Known as Company "A", Sixth Wisconsin Veteran Volunteer Infantry,* by Philip Cheek and Mair Pointon, and William Kepler's *History of the Fourth Regiment Ohio Volunteer Infantry in the War for the Union*— three unit histories typical of the large class that comes very close to being contemporary source books. But I was allowed to have my way. In the next two or three years I was able to make quite a haul, and for not very much money.

Then what happened? Lloyd Lewis published *Sherman, Fighting Prophet,* a book that demonstrated, I believe for the first time, the use that could be made of personal narratives and regimental histories. In 1951 Bruce Catton came out with *Mr. Lincoln's Army,* the first volume in his fine trilogy on the Army of the Potomac, and made even more striking use of the same kind of material. Booksellers and collectors woke up. Try to find the personal narrative and the really good regimental history—many are not worth shelf space—at the prices which I bought them for in the late thirties. You won't.

I am sure that many of these scarce books will never be rare, but they are going to become scarcer, and in many instances, I predict, harder to find than the well-publicized rarities.

Perhaps, in a talk before a group primarily interested in rare books, I should stop here. Some of you may say that in discussing merely scarce books I have already gone too far. If so, I beg your pardon, and ask your indulgence while I talk about books which should be easy to acquire—but often aren't. My justification is the assumption that no group like this can be uninterested in the general availability of books, and that you would like to see all significant books readily accessible to the scholars who need them.

To make the point I want to make, I shall have to draw on personal experience. For several years I devoted much of my free time to putting together an anthology of American history. An anthology is commonly considered to be the lowest form of hack work, yet I happen to believe that an anthology can be no less creative than original writing. It will not achieve this status, however, unless the anthologist is willing to work, which means that on any broad subject he must consult a great many books. My hardest problem turned out to be not reading the books, but finding them.

I proceeded by making lists of titles on various subjects. Take, as an example, a chapter of the book which eventually came to be called "Enjoying Life—and Learning." There I wanted to show how Americans living in the last third of the nineteenth century amused themselves and were amused and enlightened. I wanted original narratives dealing with sports, music, the theater, literature, the colleges. I found leads in many places, but principally in sources cited in general works, in special bibliographies, and in the book-review sections of such scholarly journals as the *Mississippi Valley Historical Review.* For a chapter such as the one I have mentioned I might start with a list of twenty-five books, although in the end I would look at several times that number. With a list of twenty-five I would try the Chicago Historical Society first, but there I would not be likely to find more than two or three, except in those fields in which the Society concentrates. My next resort would be the excellent library of the University of Chicago. There I would probably pick up a dozen. The Newberry Library would give me three or four of those which remained, and I might locate one or two in the Chicago Public Library. *But never once was I able to find every book on as short a list as twenty-five titles, and I usually missed four or five.*

Bear in mind two facts. I was using the combined resources of four important libraries, an aggregate book collection excelled only by Boston, Washington, and New York. And I was not, for the most part, looking for rare books. In fact, when I did want a rare book I never failed to locate it. What gave me the most trouble were books published in the last twenty-five or thirty years—often books published by university presses and the best-known trade houses. I cannot cite examples, because when I finish working on a book I throw away all my notes and working papers and try to forget the whole unpleasant business as quickly as I can. But I am not mistaken as to my facts and I assure you that I do not exaggerate.

Before this experience I had assumed that at least a fair number of large libraries would automatically order the entire list of a publisher like Alfred Knopf, excepting the juveniles, mysteries, and light fiction. Upon inquiry I was told that there are exactly two libraries which have a standing order of this kind with Knopf—Harvard and Princeton.

If my experience in book hunting was a typical one—and I am persuaded that I was more successful in Chicago than I would have been in most cities—then we are not doing as good a job as we should in preserving and making accessible the product of the American press, which is almost the same thing as the product of the American mind.

And why not? Because the cost, either in dollars or in space, would be too great? That I cannot believe. Presently some 12,000 books are published annually in the United States. Subtract from that number the reprints, the juveniles, most of the mysteries, and the genealogies (by all means the genealogies) and I think the figure will come down to 6,000. My guess is that a good many libraries are already buying 5,000 of the 6,000 titles. To complete the job such libraries would need to buy only 1,000 more books a year. Put the cost per book at $5.00, which is probably high, and the added cost comes only to $5,000. Now consider the number of libraries with annual book budgets running to six figures, and it will be seen that the financial problem is not very formidable.*

I should like to see one inclusive library in every cultural center of the country—in Ann Arbor-Detroit, in St. Louis, in Minneapolis-St. Paul, and perhaps two dozen other places. Failing something of the kind, we will not make the scholarly resources of this nation as accessible as they should be. It is of no use to say: "Oh, well, we'll borrow Thomas C. Cochran's *New York in the Confederation* (University of Pennsylvania Press, 1932) for you. Plenty of libraries will have it." They will—but generally the scholar dislikes to wait, and the business of interlibrary loan entails some expense and is a nuisance which most libraries are trying to curtail. Unless the person who asks for the Cochran book has an imperative need for it, he will probably pass it up, and his work may well suffer from the omission. We cannot, in our libraries, preserve the cultural heritage of the world in its entirety—that undertaking is too large—but we can preserve our own. And we should.

My formula for winning in the sport, or business, and sometimes I fear the racket, of book collecting, is to play

*The figures used in this paragraph are now absurdly low. P. M. A.

it across the board—to bet on the scarce and easy-to-get as well as the rare. Even then we shall not always be successful. I remember my experience at a track some years ago. In the first five races I bet to win. None of my choices came in first. The sixth race was a long one—a mile and a quarter as I remember—with only four horses entered. Lady Grey was the heavy favorite at odds of three to two. I was determined to cash a ticket even if it cost me money, so I played Lady Grey across the board. And Lady Grey came in fourth.

From that experience we may deduce a lesson. No matter how hard we try for the good books—rare, scarce, and easy-to-get—there will always be some that we'll miss.

Recollections I
New Year's Eve, 1913

A dozen years ago I came to the conclusion that the year 1913 marked a turning point in American history. So I undertook to do a book that would deal with such decisive events of the year as the beginning of the Wilson administration, the Federal Reserve Act, and the graduated income tax, as well as with such ephemeral phenomena as diaphanous skirts and *September Morn.* I thought it appropriate to conclude the book, *Crossroads, 1913,* with what a thirteen-year-old boy could remember of domestic life in the year under review.

At the beginning of this book I said that I wanted to picture the year 1913 as it unfolded before the eyes of a mature, intelligent, and inquisitive American. In closing the account, I shall draw on the recollections of an American reasonably intelligent, definitely inquisitive, but at the time, far from mature. I shall try to describe certain aspects of middle class living as I remember them, and I shall make a good many statements which, to readers of my own age, will seem to be superfluous. My contemporaries, for example, do not need to be told that there was no radio in 1913 (except for commercial and ship-to-ship communication) but I suspect that this fact will surprise a good many younger readers. And so with many other facilities and conveniences which a generation that did not see them come into existence tends to take for granted.

From *Crossroads: 1913* by Paul M. Angle. © 1963 by Rand McNally & Company

I lived in a comfortable frame house. Writing, as I am, in bitter winter weather, I am glad to recall that we had central heating—a warm air coal furnace. It was hand-fired, of course—stokers would not come until later, and oil and gas furnaces not until much later. We did not have running hot water, but hot water for baths was supplied by a huge, nickel-plated, gas-fired contrivance above the bathtub that was turned on only when needed.

In 1913 the house was illuminated by gas. Each fixture had to be individually lighted, and a supply of long wax tapers was kept for this purpose. Electricity was available for lighting (except on the farms), and many were using it, but power failures were frequent. Two or three years later, when my father remodeled our house extensively, he put in wiring but retained the gas fixtures. We often needed them.

My mother, like most housewives, cooked on a gas range—a range with the oven above the burners, where it would still be located if designers of appliances had any regard for convenience. In the summer we "took" ice, a luxury in which even many well-to-do families, which we weren't, did not indulge. (I know. In 1918 I spent the first of four summers carrying ice. In the morning my partner and I worked through one of the wealthy sections of town. We carried no more than two-thirds of the houses and the competing company served only a few of the others. In the afternoon our route took us through a working class neighborhood in which about one resident in ten was a customer. There was no mechanical refrigeration.)

In the house we had no electrical appliances—no electric iron, no vacuum cleaner, no toaster, no electric coffeemaker, no electric-powered washing machine, although embryonic versions of all five were on the market. My mother still relied on a heavy solid flatiron heated on the stove, cleaned the rugs with a Bissell carpet sweeper, made toast in the oven and coffee in an enamelware pot, and washed by hand. (Many women used a washing machine which was essentially a covered wooden tub with paddles agitated by a lever which the operator moved back and forth.) The sewing machine was driven by a treadle. Once or twice a year it was kept busy for several days by a seamstress, engaged long in advance, who did the sewing for which a busy mother could not find time.

With few exceptions, usually among the wealthy who owned carriages or automobiles, housewives ordered groceries and meat by telephone, and ordered them from separate stores. Butchers operated their own shops, unaffiliated with groceries. All stores, except dime stores, were independently owned. The one chain food store in Mansfield at this time was the Grand Union and Pacific Tea Company, which limited itself to tea, coffee, and spices. Fresh vegetables and fruits were available only in season, although such exotics as oranges, lemons, and grapes (from Spain and packed in cork) could be had in the winter holiday season. Most women canned vegetables and fruits and made their own preserves, chili sauce, and catsup even though all these commodities could be had in the stores. (Need I say that frozen foods were many years in the future?) As a rule, housewives baked their own bread, or most of it. In our family we used bakery bread, and a good product it was—of real heft and with a crisp brown crust unspoiled by wax paper. Even so, every Saturday morning my mother baked rolls, sweet rolls, pies, and a cake or two. No self-respecting cook would have depended on a commercial bakery for these.

At another place in this book I have dealt with women's dress in 1913. I have no recollection of slit skirts or peek-a-boo waists. It may be that I was not enough interested in women to notice what they wore; more probably the innovations had not yet reached the smaller cities. I do remember very clearly the male attire of the time. In essentials it had changed little for many years. All men wore long underwear, cotton in the summer, woolen in the winter. There were no light-weight summer suits. (I saw my first summer suit in 1925, when I went to live and work in Springfield, Illinois, one of the hotter localities of the country. The suit was a seersucker, which I still believe to be the coolest of summer garments.) Work shirts came with collars attached; dress shirts were made for detachable collars, of linen for the more affluent, of celluloid for those who had to economize. (The celluloid collar could be cleaned at home; the linen collar had to be sent to the laundry.) Haircuts cost a quarter and no tip, shaves fifteen cents. For women there were no beauty shops. In our town, when weddings or other important social events made beauty treatments imperative, a diminutive, respected Negress, America Spencer by name, trotted from house to house to administer them. Boys started to wear long pants when they left grade school—all, that is, except a pitiable few who were so far behind in growth that their parents would not invest in clothes certain to be outgrown soon.

At the approach of winter every owner of an automobile, at least in the North, jacked it up on blocks, drained the radiator, and reconciled himself to the fact that the car would stay in the garage, usually a former stable, until spring. In Mansfield the streets were completely devoid of automobile traffic in the winter. We lived near a long hill, perfect for sledding. For the benefit of the boys of the neighborhood the property owners on one side of the street refrained from shoveling the sidewalks after a snow. More than that, they permitted us, after school, to draw tubs of water with which we iced the trampled walks. In an hour or so we had an ideal surface, icy, fast, but rough enough that sleds could be steered. On Flexible Flyers, on old-fashioned wooden sleds with round steel runners, on a variety of bobsleds, all homemade, we coasted down that hill at speeds between thirty and forty miles an hour. There was no danger whatever of a collision with a vehicle, either horse-drawn or motor, at any of the several cross streets.

Social life was simple: some calling, especially in the summer, a picnic now and then, an occasional church supper or church-sponsored entertainment, and rarely, an evening at the Opera House to see a play or minstrel show by a touring company. There was vaudeville, but respectable people did not patronize it. My parents rarely entertained or visited friends. As a family we attended the annual Sunday School picnic, the annual grocers' picnic (much more fun), and the annual Burton Holmes travel lecture. Sunday School and church were obligatory. There was no parental objection to cards but we never played. Reading, mostly magazines, was our sole diversion. My older sister played the piano and played well, but we had no Victrola. Neither did anyone of my acquaintance.

I wish I could remember where I was when the year came to an end on the night of December 31. Since I had turned thirteen only a week earlier I must have been at home. At 10:30 or thereabouts my father would have been asleep over the *Saturday Evening Post;* my mother, up since 6:30, would have been nodding over her mending. The three young children, a girl and two boys, would have been bedded down for a couple of hours; my older sister was in Dallas, studying music. So I would have gone to the kitchen for the nightly snack: cheese—Herkimer, aged Wisconsin brick, or imported Swiss (none of your devitalized stuff in packages)—or a saucer-full of raw oysters, supplemented with pie and coffee. And then I would have gone to bed, unaware that I had just passed through a pivotal year, and without the slightest suspicion that I would ever write a book about it.

Recollections II
My Father
and the Grocery Store

When my mother died it fell to me, as the oldest son and
the one with the fewest pressing responsibilities, to close up
her small apartment and dispose of her possessions.
Among those I found several cartons of photographs,
mostly studio pictures of family groups and individuals.
But the collection also included six or eight photographs of
my father's grocery store. I well remember how these were
taken because I am in one as a clerk. An itinerant
photographer would come along and ask permission to
take pictures—no charge, no obligation. Of course he
would be back a few days later with mounted prints for
sale. I am glad that on several occasions at least my father
bought and kept the pictures. In me they aroused strong
feelings of nostalgia, and I decided to write about the store
as I remembered it. *American Heritage* published the
article, using all the pictures I had found as illustrations.
To my regret, the editors changed the title I had selected,
"My Father and the Grocery Store," to "My Father's
Grocery Store." Here I have restored the original title
because the article is as much a character sketch of John E.
Angle as it is a picture of his business as I knew it.

As I remember, I was nine years old when my father
decided that the time had come for me to "help out" in
his grocery store. The year was 1910, and the place was

Mansfield, Ohio. Twelve years would pass before I escaped completely from that thralldom.

In the beginning my duties were as small as I was: taking an occasional deposit to the bank and obtaining change, collecting small accounts, and delivering orders to customers who lived nearby and wanted a few groceries in a hurry. I also scrubbed the mold—it was harmless—from the hams and sides of bacon that hung in our back room, and from "Lebanon bologna," a wonderful smoked summer sausage which we bought in barrels, if you please, from a maker in Lebanon, Pennsylvania.

I do not remember the amount of my pay, but I suspect that I was doing a little work for the allowance I would have received in any case. And I had one compensation enjoyed by no other youngster in town. My father loved baseball, and every day the team was in town, except Saturdays and Sundays, we were in the bleachers. (On Saturdays we had too much business in the store; and on Sundays, in our family, we went only to church.) I can still remember Mansfield's first baseman, Zeke Reynolds; a third baseman named Tim Flood who had an arm about as strong as an old maid's; and a pitcher, Jeff Holmquist, who once went twenty–seven straight innings, won his game, and retired from baseball with a permanently ruined arm.

As time passed I became a kind of junior clerk, waiting on customers when my father and the two clerks were busy, putting up orders, and packaging the many commodities that we bought in bulk. (Packaging in the modern supermarket appalls me, and I cannot reconcile myself to the lavish use of paper bags. We never used one if we could avoid it. Did the customer want to carry home a purchase of six or eight articles? We sold him a basket.) There was sugar, granulated, powdered, light brown, and dark brown, to be put up in two-pound and five-pound bags; an insecticide called Slug Shot, which we sold in one-pound packages; and coffee—always coffee.

Coffee deserves special mention. My father sold Chase & Sanborn's coffees almost exclusively. We carried the premium Seal Brand, which even then came in tins, but our big seller was a Santos that we sold under the private brand of Angle's Lunch Coffee. (Twenty–five cents a pound when I first remember it.) We received it in sixty–pound bags direct from Boston, ground it in our own mill, and packaged it in purple glazed-paper bags supplied by Chase & Sanborn. We also carried Mocha, Java, and Maleberry Java in the bean. Try to find any of the three in stores today.

Tea, too, was a bulk commodity. Although we stocked Lipton's, Salada, and Chase & Sanborn's Orange Pekoe in packages, most of the tea was ladled out of a row of big canisters which stood on a shelf behind the coffee mill. We had four: one each for young hyson, oolong, gunpowder, and spider-leg Japan. In comparison with coffee we sold little tea, so incoming shipments were infrequent. But they were exciting occasions. Tea was shipped then, and may be still, in big cubic containers of paper-lined lead foil. These were covered with straw matting, bound with split bamboo, and marked with Chinese and Japanese characters. Foreign foods were no novelty in our store—we had sardines from France, Portugal, and Norway; condiments and jams from England and Scotland; grapes and raisins from Spain; bulk olives from Italy—but here, in the great packages of tea, was the mysterious East. Nothing quite equalled them.

I am sure that the store's volume, in coffee and tea, was insignificant by today's standards, but fifty years ago it was large enough to deserve careful cultivation. Every Christmas brought a substantial gift from Chase & Sanborn: an inlaid tea caddy, a silver coffee service, a silver tray. These were cherished, not so much as possessions but as evidences of a relationship that somehow seemed to transcend the merely commercial.

Our own packaging of sugar, coffee, tea, and other com-modities was prevailing trade practice. The grocery store of 1912 bore a far closer resemblance to the store of 1882, when my father first entered the business, than it did to the store of 1921, the last year of which I have direct knowledge.

In 1912 we still sold many kinds of food in bulk only. On the floor stood paper-lined bushel baskets containing navy beans, marrowfat beans, kidney beans, lima beans, dried peas, split peas, oatmeal, and rolled oats. (Oatmeal and rolled oats are not the same.) We had tubs of salt mackerel and kegs of sour, dill, and sweet pickles. Cheese came only in wheels or bricks and was not, thank God, processed. In the summer, if sales were slow, oil would begin to ooze from the last segment of a wheel of Herkimer. A day or two later maggots would appear, and simultaneously, through some kind of telepathy, our one customer who would buy cheese only when it had maggots in it. (I always wondered whether he ate maggots and all or picked them out first, but I am sure his cheese was unsurpassed in richness and pungency.)

There were times when selling bulk goods meant hard work. Vinegar, for instance. Because ours was a "quality" store we stocked vinegar in bottles—cider vinegar, tarragon, and white wine—but most of what we sold was drawn from a barrel into containers which our customers supplied.

Tapping the barrel took both skill and muscle. A full barrel weighed well over two hundred pounds. The first step in the procedure was to swing it up on end, pry out the wooden stopper, and drive in the spigot, making sure that it was turned off. Then we had to work the barrel onto a low cradle, with the spigot at the bottom of the front end and the bung at the top of the barrel.

Next came the turn of an ingenious tool. The bung starter, made of hard wood, had a head something like the head of an axe and a narrow, flat haft with just the right amount of spring to it. One hammered on the barrel around the bung, which gradually loosened. It was then wrapped in a piece of burlap and fitted lightly into the bunghole. The burlap was porous enough to admit the air that was needed before the vinegar would flow from the spigot, and yet dense enough to keep out flies and insects—or most of them.

Incidentally, in my youth the bung starter was the barkeeper's favorite weapon. Most whiskey was sold from barrels, so at least one was to be found behind every bar. Time after time, when the unmistakable sounds of riot came from the saloon next door, I have looked on the scene from the safety of the rear entrance—our store and the saloon shared a back porch—and watched one of the Wolf brothers in magnificent action, conquering the field with a bung starter. By the time the police arrived, only an ambulance was needed.

One other lively memory centers on the next-door saloon. The local breweries sold beer on credit, but every Monday morning each saloon had to pay its bill in full. A collector saw to that. By long-standing custom, he bought one for the house when the bill was paid. But here the rules were strict: the "house" meant only the customers who were present when the collector came through the swinging doors. There were five saloons around the public square on which our store was situated, and every Monday morning some artful maneuvering took place.

About ten o'clock a dozen barflies would emerge from Schmutzler's and head tentatively for the Park Saloon. Julius Weber, the collector for Renner & Weber's Brewery, would tag along behind with great deliberation. When three-fourths of the distance had been covered Mr. Weber would veer sharply to the right and head at top speed for Wolf Brothers'. Instantly the pack would change course, but Mr. Weber usually won. And so did Mr. Bricker, the collector for Mansfield's other brewery.

To return to the scoops and balance-weight scales and paper bags. . . . Selling bulk goods, as I have indicated, was trade practice, but with my father it was also the result of a strong conviction. Bulk goods, he believed—and with reason—were just as good as those that came already packaged, and always cheaper. Why make the customer pay an unnecessary premium?

Take Argo starch as an example. For many years he refused to handle it. I can still hear him say: "I have bulk starch just as good as Argo, and I can sell it at half the price." In time we came to stock Premium soda crackers and Uneeda biscuits in packages, but he always preferred to sell the Premium crackers from the tins in which they came and the Uneeda biscuits from their characteristic cottonwood boxes. (I wonder what he would think today of radishes and green onions in cellophane bags. I know what he would think—and I can almost hear him snort.)

By the time I was gently but firmly led to work, my father had been in the grocery business for almost thirty years. In his own boyhood, the same persuasion that he exercised on me had taken him into his father's grocery store, and the result was a determination to escape from it at whatever cost. The price was apprenticeship as a carriage painter.

After four years he became a master painter, armed with a certificate of competence and good character. (The document is one of my most cherished possessions.) Finding no work at his home in southern Pennsylvania, he started west, making his way, after a few months, to Mansfield, Ohio, where he had relatives. There he found work at his trade, but he was injudicious enough to fall in love with the daughter of a prominent grocer. He married the daughter, started to work in the store, and in 1882, when his father-in-law decided to go into the wholesale business, bought it.

His first act was characteristic. The store, A. W. Remy & Son, was well known. My father immediately took down the sign. While the removal was in progress Louis Freundlich, Mansfield's leading clothing merchant, walked up.

"John," he said, "you're making a mistake. Remy's is a well-known, respected name. Operate under it."

"Mr. Freundlich," my father replied, "maybe I'll succeed and maybe I'll fail, but whatever I do, I'll do under my own name."

John Angle had just that kind of quiet courage. He was a prohibitionist by strong conviction. The saloon next door served a light lunch—not free, but costing no more than ten or fifteen cents. It consisted of sandwiches and soup. Although the soup was made in a wash boiler, it was good—bean soup, split pea, or vegetable. (My father always maintained that it was purposely overseasoned so that it would lead to another beer.) Most of the ingredients for the lunch came from our store.

One day a friend came in with one of the local-option petitions that the Mansfield drys regularly and vainly circulated. (Mansfield had a large German population, and the good burghers had no intention of giving up their schnapps and beer. They didn't, until compelled to by the Eighteenth Amendment and the Volstead Act. It is ironic that the first federal Prohibition commissioner should have been Honest John Cramer, a Mansfielder.)

"John," my father's friend said, "I don't suppose you will want to sign this on account of the boys next door"—pointing to the saloon—"but I thought I'd give you a chance."

"Let me have it," my father replied, and immediately affixed his fine bold signature. The Wolf brothers, be it recorded to their credit, continued to buy split peas and cabbage and tomatoes as if nothing had happened.

The Wolfs were only two of our rather incongruous customers. Three or four doors away stood Brunk's tailor shop. There worked Mr. Mendlich—ten hours a day five days a week, and until nine at night on Saturdays. We could always count on Mr. Mendlich on Saturday night. His first stop, after work, was Wolf Brothers', where he bought two bottles of beer. Next came Angle's Grocery. Mr. Mendlich was an Austrian with a rudimentary knowledge of English.

"Da feesh," he would say, and whoever was waiting on him would fetch a quarter-pound of dried herring, "blind robbins" in our parlance. "Brod," "kase," and two or three other standard items followed—the list never varied. Mr. Mendlich, obviously, was preparing for a Saturday night lunch, his one pleasure of the week. He was a very small man, no more than four and a half feet tall, and always neatly dressed in heavy, old-fashioned European woolens; he was always pleasant and deferential. Forty-five years ago I thought him funny. Today I look on him as an admirable citizen and a complete gentleman.

And there was Phoebe Wise. Phoebe was as much a part of Mansfield's history as Johnny Appleseed, the Dowie Elders, and Senator John Sherman, and more romantic than any of them. She was a recluse who lived a short distance out of town and quite near the Ohio State Reformatory. The story was—whether true or not I never knew—that when Phoebe was a young woman she had a lover of whom her father disapproved violently. The young man could not call at the house, and had to see Phoebe surreptitiously. One night the reformatory siren wailed to announce the escape of a prisoner. Soon afterward there was a noise in the bushes near the Wise house. Phoebe's father took his shotgun and fired in the direction of the sound. Later, when he investigated, he found the dead body of his daughter's lover. Thereafter, Phoebe dressed only in the clothing she had assembled for a trousseau, and left the house only when need compelled her to.

One summer afternoon I stood in front of the store, disgustedly watching two country boys cut capers for the benefit of their girls. One had a bottle of evil-smelling medicine, which he insisted on poking under all noses. Phoebe Wise approached, dressed as always in her 1880 finery. "Hey, Phoebe!" the boy with the bottle called out. Phoebe, though slightly "touched," had dignity, and everyone treated her with consideration. "Hey, Phoebe!" the boy repeated. "What does this smell like?" Phoebe sniffed the bottle gravely, and then commented with deliberation: "To me it smells just like horse-piss." The boys and their girls retreated in red-faced confusion and Phoebe, unperturbed, made her purchases.

At the opposite end of the social and economic scale were two other customers, Mr. Leiter and Peter Scholl. Mr. Leiter was an aristocrat; at least he lived on Park Avenue, the fashionable street, and enjoyed an independent income. But the income was Mrs. Leiter's, and she was not noted for her liberality. When she sent Mr. Leiter shopping, she gave him the exact change that he would need.

Now Mrs. Leiter was a vegetarian, and so, perforce, was her husband. Yet, in the store he always managed to sidle up to the meat slicer, eyes open for any nubbin of summer sausage or slice of boiled ham that might by lying there. He thought that he snitched these morsels and wolfed them without our knowledge. We pitied Mr. Leiter. Had we known when he was coming I think we would have been prepared with something more substantial than the usual scraps.

Peter Scholl was an aristocrat, but a real one. He owned the Independent Oil Company, a distributing firm; lived in one of Mansfield's great Victorian houses; and was driven back and forth to work every day by a liveried coachman behind two of the finest bays I have ever seen. He was tall, portly, and florid, with waxed mustaches, and winter and summer he wore a Homburg and a Prince Albert coat. In appearance he resembled Bismarck, but not in manner. When he stopped at the store to buy French sardines packed in olive oil and vegetables—a delicacy that seems to have disappeared from American groceries—or greengage plums in heavy syrup, or peaches in brandy, he would deal only with my father, to whom he was as deferential as he would have been to Bismarck himself.

Peter Scholl knew, of course, that my father was his customer, although a very small one, but I wonder whether the owner of the Independent Oil Company ever knew the strength of John Angle's loyalty. We had a kerosene tank from which we sold a few gallons a week. The kerosene came from Peter Scholl's comany. At intervals a Standard Oil salesman would try to get the business, small as it was. Whatever the inducement—a big discount, a new tank free—it was rejected with comtempt.

I wish I could say that all the "carriage trade" customers were like Peter Scholl. A few were so insufferable that they aroused prejudices in me from which I have never escaped— prejudices which, in fact, I cherish. They were the ones who drove around in White Steamers, belonged to the country club, played golf, said "marasheeno" instead of "maraskeeno" and "tomahto" instead of "tomayto," were alternately imperious and condescending with all of us at the store, and rarely paid their bills on time. I have never joined a country club, I gave up golf after one brief whirl, I say "maraskeeno" and "tomayto," I treat clerks with courtesy, and I pay my bills promptly. . . . Page a psychiatrist.

In happy contrast were the Canarys. Tom Canary was a "white-wing"—he swept up the horse droppings from the streets around the square. His route took him past the store, and he frequently stopped to place an order. Whenever possible, I delivered it, because I found the sight of old Mrs. Canary smoking a corncob pipe endlessly fascinating. To this day, I have seen no other woman indulge in this pleasure.

Mrs. Canary smoked Five Brothers tobacco. I doubt that

the brand is still on the market. And what, I wonder, has happened to some of our other steady sellers—Star Brand plug, Red Band and Mail Pouch scrap, fine-cut under any name, and Bull Durham and Duke's Mixture? I say nothing of cigarettes: in Ohio the seller had to pay a stiff license fee, and the demand, before World War I, was too small to justify our handling them.

I look back, with mixed feelings, on another element of our business: the sale of Fourth of July fireworks. We stocked heavily: torpedoes, firecrackers, cannon crackers ranging in length from two to twelve inches, grasshoppers, Roman candles, sky rockets, pinwheels, fountains, and relatively harmless sparklers. Part of our stock was displayed in the front windows of the store and part on sidewalk tables. Since the clerks and my father were usually busy inside, I took care of the sidewalk.

There, for ten days, I would alternate between excitement and fear. To sell fireworks was fun, but to watch men paw through Roman candles with one hand while the other hand held a lighted cigar—that was not fun. Moreover, the mild admonitions of a twelve-year-old boy had little influence on adults. We escaped accident only through good luck.

This was the bad side of fireworks; the good side came out on Fourth of July night. Since my father was able to buy at cost, he always laid in for his family a more lavish assortment of fireworks than anyone else in the neighborhood. On the whole, it was his show. The children, under close surveillance, were allowed to wave sparklers, and the older ones were trusted with an occasional Roman candle, but it was my father who nailed the pinwheels to the fine hard maples that bordered the street in front of our house and fired the sky rockets from a specially constructed trough. The display was memorable, and no one was ever hurt.

The Fourth of July, in my boyhood, had only two rivals in the calendar of events. One was the annual grocers' picnic. The great day approached at snail's speed, but it never failed to arrive. At 7 A.M. the town's grocers and clerks, their wives and families, with heavily laden picnic baskets, boarded a Baltimore & Ohio special train for Sandusky, fifty miles

north on Lake Erie. By nine o'clock the train had reached
its destination, and everyone ran up the gangplank of the
old side-wheeler that plied between the city and Cedar Point,
three miles across the bay.

Fifty years ago the Point was paradise. (It may still be.)
For excitement it offered a huge roller coaster, for the "fast"
set it provided a dance hall and wine rooms, where the
very good wines of the Lake Erie islands could be bought
by the glass; but for everyone from the land-locked city
of Mansfield the great attraction was a marvelous beach
sloping so gently that even small children could wade far
out in safety. Here our family spent most of the day, the
women dressed in middy blouses with long sleeves, baggy
bloomers, and long black stockings; the men and boys almost
as amply clothed. (I wonder where we changed. I don't
remember bathhouses.)

About dusk, and all too soon, came departure time. Once
more the trip across the bay, then the boarding of the B&O
special. Many of the picnickers, tired out because unaccus-
tomed to sun and water and stuffed with the contents of
the baskets, would curl up to sleep. They rarely succeeded.
There were always some who had underestimated the
strength of the island wines or overestimated their own
capacities, so the return trip was at best noisy, and at worst
marked by a few brawls. But these were incidents readily
overlooked even by our abstinent family. Nothing could mar
the pleasures of the grocers' picnic. Even the weather was
beneficent. I do not remember a rainy day.

The other great day was Christmas, which I suppose I
looked forward to with especial zest because it was my
birthday. But for the joys of Christmas I paid a price. There
were two hundred Christmas trees to be boxed, and I was
a helper, though not a willing one. My father had discovered
years before my time that by nailing trees in boxes, which
served as standards, he could get larger sales and higher
prices. All year long he saved the fine white pine packing
cases in which all canned goods were delivered. The trees
would arrive about the time my Christmas vacation began,
and from then until the twenty-fourth of December I would

be busy with hammer and saw.

I was fatuous enough to think that I would escape this chore when I went to college. I didn't. I sometimes suspect that boxing Christmas trees, like my experience with some of Mansfield's elite, left me with a psychosis. Never since have I touched the simplest carpenter's tools except under urgent necessity.

The Christmas-tree trade was my last experience with the grocery store. In fact, my days as a clerk ended with the summer of 1917, after I had finished my junior year in high school. For three months I worked full-time. I opened the store at 6 A.M. A few minutes later the truck gardener appeared, his wagon loaded with vegetables of a freshness rarely encountered today: green onions, green turnips, kohlrabi (who now knows kohlrabi?), radishes (especially the slender white icicles), carrots, leaf lettuce, green and wax beans that really snapped, peas in pods that crackled when opened—all pulled no later than the preceding afternoon. As the summer advanced, sweet corn came on the market— first the Early Evergreen, then the scraggly but delicious Golden Bantam with its big yellow kernels in four double rows and the wonderful Country Gentleman whose kernels didn't grow in rows, and finally the large white Stowell's Evergreen, lord of all the sweet corns. No hybrids these, but the true varieties, with a flavor and a succulence lost forever.

All summer there were berries: strawberries, blackberries, black raspberries, red raspberries, and huckleberries shipped from the Cumberland Valley of Pennsylvania, my father's boyhood home. These were his special care. For hours each day he would stand at a counter, turning each quart from its original wooden box into a new one. In the process he would pick out any that were soft or mouldy. At the same time the larger ones managed to land on top, and somehow the thirty-two quarts of the standard crate became thirty-four quarts. In the winter, by similar necromancy, the contents of a container of bulk oysters expanded in the same proportion.

The vegetables, the berries, the tomatoes, the cantaloupe

and watermelons, the peaches and pears and plums and early apples that appeared before the end of the summer, were offered for sale not inside the store but in front of it. The fruits were displayed in bushel baskets, berries and garden vegetables were ranged on long tables, and watermelons made a row near the curb.

In the winter the same outdoor tables held smoked sausage and fresh sausage in the gut—far superior to the stuff that comes in cloth bags—pudding meat, souse, and head cheese, all produced by local farmers. Spring saw the tables loaded with sassafras root and Richland County maple syrup, at least the equal of the more famous products from the Western Reserve and Vermont.

My working day, that summer of 1917, lasted from 6 A.M. until 6 P.M. Until 6 P.M., that is, on Tuesday, Wednesday, Thursday, and Friday. On Monday, for some historic reason which no one remembered, we stayed open until 9 P.M.; on Saturday until 11 P.M. My father, as reluctant a riser as I am, arrived at the store between 7:30 and 8 o'clock in the morning. Even in my time he had given up the Monday night stint—there was little business—but on Saturday night he stayed to shut up shop. This meant balancing the cash register, computing his personal grocery bill for the week, making a final inspection, and examining the fruits and berries to see whether there were any which could not be expected to survive until Monday. Those which looked doubtful he took home, and on Sunday afternoon my mother converted them into preserves or canned them.

Arriving home about midnight, my father embarked on a program that never varied. First, he bathed and shaved in preparation for church the following morning. Then he dressed, at least to the extent of trousers and undershirt. Next, he addressed himself to a snack. If oysters were in season, he would have half a pint raw, seasoned with vinegar and salt and pepper. For the rest of the year his preference was cove oysters (in cans) or his best sardines. Following the first course came half of one of the pies my mother had baked that morning, and then three or four cups of coffee. The food gone, he read the *Saturday Evening Post* until, in spite of the coffee, he found himself nodding. And so to bed. I doubt that the most ardent concertgoer, the most dedicated devotee of the theatre, ever found more pleasure in music or the stage than my father derived from his simple Saturday indulgences.

The pre-supermarket grocery store called for long hours and hard work. Ours, at least, yielded only a modest return. The peak of my father's earnings came during and after World War I, when he netted, without charging anything for his own services, about $5,000 a year. In the 1920s, chain-store competition began to hurt. Business dropped off, yet he managed, with the invaluable aid of my mother, who worked harder even than he did, to maintain a large house, feed the family well, and bring the last of eight children to maturity. When he sold the store in 1939, after fifty-seven years, it was no forced sale, but one dictated by an arthritic condition which made long hours on his feet impossible. And I am proud to say that all his bills were paid, and that he ended up with a small surplus.

Recollections III
The Blue Danube

This little reminiscence needs no prefatory comment. It is one of a series of short articles, entitled "North Avenue Vignettes," I wrote on the changing neighborhood of which the Chicago Historical Society is a part.

I am a little hazy about my first acquaintance with the Blue Danube, but since at least twenty-five years have passed since that happy event I hope I will be forgiven. I think my initiation took place shortly before 1945, when I came to Chicago with my family. As I recall it, someone had recommended the Blue Danube as an unpretentious night club where one could spend a couple pleasant hours for a modest amount of money. On this first evening I appealed to a taxi driver, who happened to be knowledgeable and took me to a simple one-story building on the corner of North and Hudson avenues. There I found enchantment.

This was my first experience with Hungarian gypsy music. I had never seen nor heard a cymbalon, that marvellous instrument which, sounded by hammers, combines the twang of the harpsichord with the lower strings of the guitar. But the cymbalon player, expert as he was, paled before the violinist. Never before and rarely since have I heard music such as Béla Babai could evoke from a fiddle. A second violinist added only volume to the music. Certainly he contributed nothing to its verve.

The dancing, too, was new to me. The patrons were nearly all Hungarians or of Hungarian descent, and they knew

From *Chicago History*, Spring 1971, pp. 156–57.

the old country dances. Pairing off, men and women put their hands on each others' shoulders and moved slowly through the mournful opening bars of the gypsy songs. Suddenly the little orchestra swung into the fast tempo of the csárdás and the dancers swung each other around and stamped their heels in a pandemonium of exuberance.

After a year and a half in Chicago we found a house, only four blocks, easy walking distance, from the Blue Danube. After that we were regular patrons. Neither the management nor the waitresses were concerned that my two children were under the legal drinking age—no question was ever raised when the four of us consumed two bottles of wine. With four pork chop sandwiches, and a couple thimbles of that marvellous Hungarian apricot brandy, Barack Pálinka, the check might run to $12.00.

Far too soon the Blue Danube had to yield to progress. A building and loan association bought the corner, and the night club went out of business. For a few months Béla and his little orchestra played at Caruso's on Rush Street, but there they were misfits. One night we went there for dinner expressly to hear them. For half an hour I listened to as dull music as I had ever heard—I found it incredible that Béla's talent had declined so far. In a few minutes two good-looking, well-dressed young women came in and took seats in the front row of the little concert room. Béla's brown eyes sparkled and immediately his violin sang as it always had.

From Chicago, Béla Babai went to play at a Hungarian restaurant called the Csardash in New York City. Every time I have been in New York and had the opportunity I have spent an hour or two there. He always recognized me as being from Chicago. On my last visit, about two years ago, I visited the Csardash, accompanied by my wife, my daughter, and her husband. No, Béla would not be there that night: he was not well, and played only twice a week. But tomorrow would be one of his nights. Would we come back? We would—and did. Béla greeted us at once. "Chicago," he said, "and you lived around North Park and Menomonee." (He hit the location on the nose.) And then he played as

I had rarely heard him play before. I knew the reason. My daughter is as pretty as she was as a college girl, and he was playing only for her, just as he had played only for the two dolls at Caruso's fifteen years earlier.

A long time ago, on our first trip to Mexico City, my wife and I had dinner at a Hungarian restaurant. The simple entertainment featured a gypsy fiddler and a good one, Señor Golwoertz. Before we left I went up to buy one of his records. On an impulse I asked: "Have you ever heard of Béla Babai?" "Béla Babai?" he answered. "Chicago? The greatest of all gypsy fiddlers!"

I only hope that Béla still plays at the Csardash and delights the patrons with the plaintive and wild songs of the Hungarian plains.

My Own, My Native Land

As the Inland Steel Company approached its seventy-fifth anniversary I was asked to write an article on the agricultural and industrial development of the Middle West for the company's excellent publication, *Inland: The Magazine of the Middle West*. I chose to embellish the straight historical account with an expression of my own feelings about the region in which I have spent my life.

> I was born in the Middle West. Such formal education as I possess I have obtained in Middle Western schools and colleges. Except for one brief aberration I have lived here all my life, and I do not think I could be happy in any other part of the country—or, for that matter, in any other part of the world. In view of these facts the reader should not expect to find a high degree of objectivity in what follows. I shall try not to distort the truth, but I cannot help writing of my own section with pride and affection.

What is there about the Middle West that sets it apart from other regions of the country? The answer might be climate, with extremes of summer heat and winter cold; but the climate is not too dissimilar from the East, and the Plains states are often hotter in summer and colder in winter. Perhaps the face of the land? If the Middle West were all prairie country, like most of Illinois, that would be a distinctive feature, but it isn't. Rugged hills mark the landscape in eastern Ohio, southern Indiana, and southern Illinois, and large

From *Inland: The Magazine of the Middle West*, Spring 1968, pp. 11–18 parts of the area are rolling. The people? Here a point could be made. Probably no other section of the country contains as many inhabitants of foreign birth or ancestry, a mixture to which large numbers of Negroes have been added since the First World War. But since immigration was restricted in 1921, ethnic differences have diminished and the population has reached a high degree of homogeneity. Often Hans Schmidt, the third generation German, can speak only a dozen words of the language—a sad loss, in my opinion—and has only a mild sentimental regard for the old country. First of all he is an American, and if he lives in Chicago, or Milwaukee, or Cincinnati, he is likely to be defiantly proud of the city of his residence.

But there are two features of the Middle West that, in combination, set it apart from the rest of the country: its magnificent farms and its great industries. Note that I have used the phrase, "in combination." New England and the Atlantic states have great industries, but their farms cannot compare with those of Ohio, Indiana, Iowa, and Illinois. The South has much rich agricultural land and produces, in cotton, one of the country's great crops, but in spite of growth in recent years its industries cannot challenge those of the North for first place. The reader may make his own evaluation of the other regions, and I prefer that he would, but I think my point will be conceded.

I begin this story with Middle Western farming, if for no other reason than that the farms came first. And I must begin many thousand years in the past, when tremendous walls of ice moved south from the arctic. Four times they advanced, reaching the Ohio River at the Ohio–Indiana line, and pushing along the Mississippi almost to the southern tip of Illinois. The last glacier, the Wisconsin, receded about 12,000 years ago, leaving behind it moraines and other deposits of drift still clearly visible.

The glaciers changed the landscape, planing off hills, filling valleys, and leaving a land of level surfaces and gentle slopes. As they melted they deposited thick layers of the fine-ground rock they had carried with them. Gradually the rock-sand decomposed. Plants and grasses took life in it, decayed and grew again, and deep soil of wonderful fertility resulted.

Slowly the forest returned, the conifers mingling with birch to cover the northern areas, the hardwoods finding their habitat farther south. But the forest stopped in western Indiana, leaving Illinois and Iowa to the vast expanses of grassland that the French explorers called prairies. Early travelers grew lyrical at the sight these unforested reaches offered. In the summer the grasses, intermingled with wild flowers, stood as high as the head of a man and rippled into waves; in the winter the brown barrenness was awesome. And when the dry prairie, touched off by lightning, took fire, the leaping flames sped faster than a horse could run, smoke rose in heavy clouds, and night became day.

Although French explorers and missionaries penetrated the Middle West in the seventeenth century, and France claimed sovereignty over much of the region for well over a hundred years, settlement never amounted to more than a few scattered missions and drowsy villages in Michigan, Wisconsin, and Illinois. "Of material results of the French regime," the historian Theodore C. Pease wrote, "it is vain to inquire: a few oddly shaped landholdings, a few peculiar titles to be fitted into a world of township surveys and Anglo-Saxon land laws, a few names of places." He was writing of Illinois, but his summation applied equally to the other places where the French tried in vain to strike roots.

After the French and Indian War the Middle West passed to Great Britain, and with the Revolution, to the United States. With peace, the great western movement of the American people began in earnest. Land, rich land for little or nothing, lay beyond the Alleghenies. Pioneers trudged over the trails and floated down the rivers to Tennessee and Kentucky, and soon to Ohio. New Englanders founded Marietta in 1788. Cincinnati began life as Losantiville in the same year. By 1803 Ohio had a population large enough for statehood and entered the Union. Indiana followed in 1816, Illinois in 1818. Michigan and Wisconsin filled up much more slowly, and did not become states until 1837 and 1848. Iowa, the twenty-ninth state, was admitted in 1846.

Everywhere in the Middle West the process of settlement

was much the same. Elias Pym Fordham, a young English civil engineer who came to Illinois in 1818, wrote a classic description. He distinguished four classes of settlers:

1st. The hunters, a daring, hardy race of men, who live in miserable cabins, which they fortify in times of War with the Indians, whom they hate but much resemble in dress and manners . . . They raise a little Indian corn, pumpkins, hogs, and sometimes have a Cow or two, and two or three horses belonging to each family, but their rifle is their principal means of support. . . . This class cannot be called first Settlers, for they move every year or two.

2nd class. First settlers, a mixed set of hunters and farmers. They possess more property and comforts than the first class; yet they are a half barbarous race. They follow the range pretty much; selling out when the Country begins to be well settled, and their cattle cannot be entirely kept in the woods.

3rd class.—is composed of enterprising men from Kentucky and the Atlantic States. This class consists of Young Doctors, Lawyers, Storekeepers, farmers, mechanics, etc., who found towns, trade, speculate in land, and begin the fabric of Society. . . . Such are the inhabitants of the Southern parts of Indiana, and of Shawanoe Town. . . .

4th class—old settlers, rich, independent farmers, wealthy merchants, possessing a good deal of information, a knowledge of the world, and an enterprising spirit.

Such were the Ohio men, western Pennsylvanians, Kentuckians, and Tennesseeans.

The key figure in settlement, the indispensable agent, was the pioneer farmer. He outnumbered all other classes by a wide margin; without him they would have been nothing. His life was hard. First of all he had to erect, with the help of a few neighbors, a log cabin. Then, in most parts of the Middle West, he had to clear his first field. This meant felling trees, cutting them up, and piling branches and trunks in heaps until they became dry enough to burn. The first crop, usually corn, was planted by dropping seeds in a furrow turned by a plow. Even in Illinois the first settlers were reluctant to venture into the prairies—marshy swamps from April until July. The soil, they reasoned, was too poor to support trees: How could it grow crops? Besides, the early settler was dependent upon wood for his cabin and sheds, for his fences, and for his fires.

For a generation the farmer could expect little more than subsistence. Unless he lived near a navigable stream there was little advantage to him in raising a surplus. The roads were atrocious, and the cost of wagon freight high. Why plant and cultivate a big crop when it would cost more to haul it to one of the growing cities, where a market existed, than it would sell for? As late as 1845 a noted agriculturist, Solon Robinson, asserted that there was an abundance of uncultivated land, as fine farm land as existed anywhere in the country, "within gun shot of the Illinois capitol."

Farmers near the rivers were more fortunate. They could butcher their hogs, cure the meat, and float it downstream on rafts or flatboats to the great market at New Orleans. Young Abraham Lincoln made two such trips as a hired hand, one from south-western Indiana and the other from central Illinois by way of the Sangamon and Illinois rivers. But this commerce was always a gamble. A flatboat could be swamped and sunk by a passing steamer. Or one could arrive at New Orleans only to find the market glutted, and prices abysmally low.

The plight of the farmer, and the small-town merchant as well, led to the craze for building canals and railroads in the 1830s.

The success of the Erie Canal, opened in 1825 between Albany and Buffalo, exceeded all expectations. The canal carried bulk products—salt, wool, cotton, grain, lumber, hemp—in greater quantities than expected; Easterners flocked westward to develop the country along its route and to contribute to the settlement of northern Illinois, Michigan, and Wisconsin; both freight and people fed the young steamboat lines on the Great Lakes. Dazzled by this example, Middle Western states undertook to build canals of their own. Ohio completed a canal between Cleveland and Portsmouth on the Ohio River in 1832, and began another in the western part of the state to link the Maumee River with Cincinnati. But the Panic of 1837, one of the most severe the country has ever experienced, delayed completion until 1845. On Indiana's one canal, planned to extend from Toledo to Terre Haute on the Wabash, work had to be suspended because of the dearth of money after the panic, but the canal went into operation between Toledo and Lafayette in 1843. Work on the Illinois and Michigan Canal, joining Chicago with the Illinois River at Peru, was dropped for several years, with the result that the first boat did not pass through until 1848.

Although the Middle Western canals never lived up to the expectations of their proponents, they played a larger role in the economy than one would suspect from the few stretches of weed-grown channels and rotting wooden locks that have survived. The canals opened new markets to the farmer, diverting grain and other products from St. Louis and New Orleans to the ports of the Great Lakes. Their era was short but while it lasted they were an important factor in developing the states of the lower Middle West.

While thousands of laborers, principally Irish immigrants, scooped out canal beds with picks and shovels, other thousands worked on railroad roadbeds. The Baltimore and Ohio had broken ground in 1828, the Charleston and Hamburg in South Carolina later in the same year. At first the cars were horse-drawn, but within two years steam locomotives were installed. In the 1830s numerous local lines were projected in the East and some were built, but here again, as with the canals, the Panic of 1837 dried up funds, and many a line never came closer to completion than a few miles of trackless right-of-way.

The first railroad in the Middle West was the Erie and Kalamazoo, which had one steam engine and ran trains between Toledo and Adrian, Michigan, in the summer of 1837. The Northern Cross, beginning at Meredosia on the

Illinois River, was finished as far as Jacksonville on January 1, 1840, and extended to Springfield early in 1842. But the effects of the panic lasted for years, with the result that no important railroad went into operation before 1847, when the Indianapolis and Madison, eighty-six miles long, connected the Indiana capital and the Ohio River. By the end of that year the Middle West possessed 660 miles of track, all, except for the Indianapolis and Madison, scattered among small local lines. But once fairly started, railroad building went with a rush. By the end of 1860, on the eve of the Civil War, trackage had increased to 9514 miles, a third of the total of the United States. Of the situation at this time the historian of the frontier, Frederic L. Paxson, could write: "The Northwest was covered with a close-meshed railroad net that brought good transportation within hauling distance of nearly every occupied farm." Now the farmer could sell all he could produce.

Thanks to three inventions, he could produce crops beyond his dreams of only twenty-five years earlier. In 1837 John Deere, a skilled blacksmith, left his native Vermont to settle in the little town of Grand Detour on the Rock River. There he soon learned that the cast iron plows made in the East worked badly in the sticky prairie soil. Within a year he and his partner, Leonard Andrus, made three plows in which they replaced the conventional iron mouldboard with a sheet of steel shaped over wood. The new plow was an immediate success, and within eight years the shop was turning out a thousand annually. In 1846 Deere sold out to Andrus and moved to Moline, where he founded the great farm implement company that bears his name today. His invention, soon adopted by other makers, expedited plowing and made it easier. (The steel plow was not, as many today assume, a plow for breaking the prairies. Its advantage was that it cut through the soil easily, and by scouring itself, relieved the farmer of the necessity of stopping every few yards to clean the share.)

On the heels of the steel plow the reaper invaded the Middle West. In the 1830s Cyrus Hall McCormick, of Rockbridge County, Virginia, had developed a practical though far from perfect reaper. After trying for several years to produce the machine through licensees he decided to manufacture it himself. Sensing that the Middle West would be the great grain-growing region of the future, he erected his plant in Chicago in 1847. Within three years he had built a national business. Competitors produced machines of their own, often infringing upon his patents, but he remained first in the field. The reaper, whether McCormick's or that of one of his rivals, resulted in a higher crop yield with less labor and at smaller cost. Within a few years its value would be demonstrated conclusively: During the Civil War it enabled the North to send many thousands of farm boys to the armies and still feed the people at home and export grain to Europe.

The third great agricultural invention was the threshing machine, which supplanted the flail and fanning mill for small grain. Although primitive threshers had been developed in Scotland in the eighteenth century, the first low-priced, efficient thresher-separators made their appearance in the 1840s. One of the leaders was Jerome I. Case of Racine, Wisconsin; another was Hiram Pitts, who began manufacturing threshers at Alton, Illinois, in 1847, and four years later moved his plant to Chicago. Like the steel plow and the reaper, the thresher increased production and lowered costs.

By the late 1850s, through the multiplication of canals and railroads and the application of machinery, the farmers of the Middle West had attained maturity. Acres formerly allowed to lie fallow were put into production, and farm owners built comfortable houses and substantial barns. Many attained wealth. Proof may be found in the county histories and atlases that flooded the region in the 1870s. They are quaint books, written by corps of hacks, but they contain biographies of thousands of successful citizens whose life stories are recorded only in those pages. Many were farmers. Here, for example, we meet Jabez Cook, who came to Richland County, Ohio, in 1815 and settled on a quarter-section that his father had entered. The country was then a wilderness and Indians were still numerous. Cook built a cabin and cleared a farm. In 1873 the biographer wrote: "It is one of the finest farms in the county, and has been awarded the premium by the County Agricultural Society." After living on the farm for thirty-nine years Cook sold it to his son and moved to Mansfield, where he invested in city lots and became a wealthy man.

Robert Cass was brought to Sangamon County, Illinois, in 1828, when he was seven years old. At eleven he began a five–year apprenticeship as a farm hand. During that time he managed to save enough money to enter forty acres, which he began to farm when he was sixteen. By the early 'seventies he owned 1000 acres. "This is a big achievement, considering his embarrassed circumstances in the beginning," the anonymous biographer wrote. "When he and his wife commenced housekeeping, all their household goods were rolled to their door on a wheelbarrow. Now they reside on as fine a farm as is in the township in which they live, well improved, and tastefully ornamented."

I could cite hundreds of examples like these two, but I shall content myself with one more. Christopher Holdeman came to Indiana from Ohio in 1839 and settled in Elkhart County. On the authority of the county atlas, "there he lived for about three months in a *rail pen,* and then built a log cabin, where he remained till the erection of his present farm mansion. He owns a fine farm, and his annual crops range from sixteen to thirty-five acres of wheat, from twelve to eighteen acres of corn, and from five to seven acres of oats." What is more William Henry Holdeman, one of Christopher's eight children, was then (1873) a student at Hillsdale College preparing to be a teacher. The biographer concluded: "He is a member of the Alpha Kappa Phi Society." There, in a sentence, you have it: from log cabin to college fraternity in one generation.

I have shown, I hope, that the first great industries of the Middle West—the plow factories, the manufacturing of reapers and threshing machines—developed in response to the needs of the farmers. At the same time an earlier industry, also stemming directly from agriculture, was taking great strides. That was pork packing. As early as 1841 Cincinnati had sixty-two beef and pork slaughterhouses, forty-eight pork packing plants, and handled 200,000 hogs a year. The size of the operation earned the city the nickname of "Porkopolis." By 1848 the number of hogs packed jumped to 500,000. But the packing industry, though dominant, was not alone. Cincinnati factories turned out soap and candles, woolen and cotton goods, linseed oil, iron castings, steam engines, wood and tinware, boots and shoes, and dozens of other articles that we have come to lump under the term, consumer goods. By 1850 the city had become the brewing and distilling capital of the world.

The industries of Cincinnati, in 1850 the great manufacturing center of the Middle West, had common characteristics. All, including the packing plants, were small, employing at most a few dozen "hands," and all were essentially craft operations. This could be said of the small shops and factories to be found everywhere in the Middle West. In 1841, for example, Cleveland (quoting the *Ohio Gazetteer* of that year) had "2 steam engine shops, 1 iron foundry, 1 sash factory, 1 brewery, 1 steam flouring mill capable of making 120 barrels of flour daily, 1 chair factory, and 3 cabinet shops." In the late 1830s in the village of Granville, Licking County, Ohio, an iron furnace and flour mill were in operation, and small factories turned out tinware, kitchen clocks, hats, cast-iron plows, furniture, brushes, boots, shoes, and rope. Springfield, Illinois, in the 1850s, had flour mills, packing plants, two woolen mills, a clothing factory, a carriage and wagon shop, three foundries, seven brickyards, and several hatters and shoemakers.

But the great industries of the Middle West were not to stem from such beginnings as these. Along with the farms, the expanding railroads provided a market that challenged innovators and men of foresight and courage. In 1857 Captain E. B. Ward established the Chicago Rolling Mill for the purpose of re-rolling iron bars into rails. In 1865 the same company began to produce steel rails, a great improvement. Two years later George M. Pullman organized the Pullman Palace Car Company with a capital of $1,000,000, and soon had cars rolling over 15,000 miles of road.

Developments like these resulted in a huge demand for iron and steel. From colonial days iron had been produced from local deposits in New Jersey, Pennsylvania, and New York. As early as 1820, Ohio smelters, exploiting indigenous "bog iron" and using charcoal for fuel, were producing considerable quantities of iron. Twenty years later it was found that coal, plentiful along the Ohio River, was a superior fuel, and production increased markedly. Not until the 1860s and 1870s, however, with the discovery of the immense sources of high grade ore in the Marquette and Menominee ranges in Michigan, did the industry approach anything like modern proportions. The ore could be shipped cheaply to north-eastern Ohio, where it met high-grade coal mined in that state and in western Pennsylvania. Although Pittsburgh remained the center of iron and steel making, Cleveland became important. The first report of its board of trade, published in 1866, listed blast furnaces, forges, and rolling mills with a capital of $3,000,000 and employing 3000 men. By 1870 the city's population had increased to 93,000, twice what it had been in 1860. Moreover, through its docks huge amounts of ore passed to Youngstown and the Mahoning Valley area, second, in Ohio, only to the lake port in the production of iron and steel.

Another natural resource, discovered about the same time as the Michigan iron ore deposits, contributed to Ohio as the industrial center of the Middle West. John D. Rockefeller of Cleveland, a young commission merchant, was one of the first to see the possibilities in the oil that had been pouring from the ground in western Pennsylvania since E. L. Drake brought in his first well in the summer of 1859. In 1863 Rockefeller concluded that Cleveland, located on two railroads and with access to the Erie Canal, could dominate the oil refining business. With four associates he built a refinery on the Cuyahoga River. Two years later he bought out three of his partners. By the end of 1865 his was the largest of Cleveland's thirty refineries. Early in 1870 he incorporated the Standard Oil Company of Ohio. By a combination of efficiency, railroad rebates, and an ability to trade blow for blow in a fiercely competitive business, plus Rockefeller's imagination and mastery of detail, Standard Oil became the giant of the refiners.

Late in the nineteenth century the steel industry began to move west. It already had a nucleus in Illinois where, in 1864, the North Chicago Rolling Mill had produced the first Bessemer steel in the United States. By 1875 the state had eleven large furnaces using bituminous coal and coke as fuel, and nine rolling mills, chiefly for producing rails. In that year Illinois turned out almost twenty-five percent of the rails rolled in the country, ranking second only to Pennsylvania.

The position of Illinois as a steel producer was strengthened in 1889, when four Illinois mills and one in Milwaukee were consolidated to form the Illinois Steel Company. The following year the 10,000 employees of this company turned out 680,274 tons of iron and steel. In 1893 Joseph Block, a Cincinnati scrap-steel merchant, bought the idle plant of the bankrupt Chicago Steel Works and with a syndicate of seven other men and $65,000 in borrowed money, formed the Inland Steel Company at Chicago Heights, Illinois. In the first six months of 1894 Inland produced a few thousand tons of finished steel—a little more than it makes in two hours today.

The great impetus to the westward movement of the steel industry came soon after the formation of the Unites States Steel Corporation in 1901. Elbert H. Gary, president of the largest industrial corporation the world had yet known, saw the advantages of a location west of the Pittsburgh and eastern Ohio area. The Middle West offered the fastest growing market in the country; it had easy access by water to the ore of Minnesota's fabulously rich Mesabi Range, opened only a few years earlier; and the fine coking coals of Pennsylvania and Ohio were not far distant. For a location, Gary and his associates chose a desolate stretch of sand dunes at the southern tip of Lake Michigan in Lake County, Indiana. The purchase was made in 1905. Within two years, 500 houses and two steel plants, one to produce steel and the other to roll it into sheet and tin plate, were under construction. The site was a few miles southeast of the Indiana Harbor location where Inland had built a new plant and poured its first steel ingots in 1902.

Today, and for some years past, the Chicago steelmaking district, comprising the contiguous area in northwestern Indiana and northeastern Illinois, produces more steel than any other similar region of the country.

While the steel industry shifted to the west, a new industry took its first faltering steps. The Duryea brothers, Charles and Frank, produced the first successful American automobile in 1893. Three years later Henry Ford built his first car. A Michigan farm boy born in 1863, Ford had become interested in internal combustion engines when he was in his twenties. While he stumbled along as a watch salesman and then as an engineer for the Edison Illuminating Company he continued to tinker with engines. In 1899 he became manager and chief engineer of the Detroit Automobile Company; four years later he organized the Ford Motor Company.

The coachwork of the early automobiles was patterned upon that of horse-drawn carriages. For this reason the new industry gravitated toward such cities as Flint, Pontiac, Lansing, and Detroit in Michigan, and South Bend, Indiana, which had long produced fine vehicles. Here the carriage shops had abundant supplies of hardwoods and plenty of expert craftsmen. Quickly Michigan—and especially the Detroit area—became the center of automobile production, and continued to hold that distinction after manufacturers turned to metal frames.

In its early years the automotive industry grew with amazing celerity. In 1900 twelve firms turned out 4000 cars— "machines," as they were often called at that time; by 1910 there were sixty-nine companies in the field and annual production jumped to 181,000. Most of these firms operated on incredibly small capital. The Ford Motor Company started business with a capital of $100,000, of which only $28,000 had been paid in. Ford survived the handicap; most of the early companies failed because of it.

The first big step in the inevitable elimination of small manufacturers came in 1908, when William C. Durant put

General Motors together. The corporation was an immediate success, but for years it remained in second place. In the year of its formation Ford introduced the Model T—sturdy, low-priced, and easy to maintain. Five years later the company perfected the continuous assembly line, with startling results. In 1912 the best Ford record for stationary chassis assembly had been 728 minutes of one man's work; by the end of 1913 the time had been cut to ninety-three minutes. Ford production jumped accordingly: from 78,440 Model T's in 1911–12 to 248,307 in 1913–14.

The next big step in consolidation came with the formation of the Chrysler Corporation. Walter P. Chrysler, an able railroad superintendent, entered the automobile business in 1912 when he became works manager of the Buick Motor Company. Four years later he moved up to the presidency. Soon afterward he switched to Willys-Overland and then to the Maxwell Motor Company, where he introduced many engineering and design improvements. In 1925 the Maxwell Motor Company became the Chrysler Corporation, which increased its slice of the market three years later by acquiring Dodge Brothers.

Most readers will not need to be told that in a field where there were once two hundred manufacturers there are now only four—the Big Three and the much smaller American Motors. Ford, General Motors, and Chrysler have plants all over the country, but the Middle West remains the center of the industry.

Akron, Ohio, became the rubber capital of the world almost by accident. Soon after the Civil War, Benjamin Franklin Goodrich, a physician who had served in the Army of the Potomac, gave up his profession to become a manufacturer of rubber, in which he saw a great future. After failing to make a success of two small companies in New York State he saw a promotional pamphlet put out by the Akron Board of Trade, and decided to build a factory there. Demand for rubber was limited to waterproof garments, fire hose, and belting, and Goodrich had hard going for ten years. However, by 1880 the B. F. Goodrich Company was firmly established, and had made Akron the center to which other rubber manufacturers—Goodyear, Firestone, and Seiberling—gravitated.

With the great expansion of the automobile industry Akron became a boom town. Between 1910 and 1920 the population jumped from 69,000 to 209,000. In one year, 1916, 30,000 workers converged on the city. Of course the rate of growth tapered off, and Akron saw hard times in the 1930s, but in spite of setbacks it was securely established as one of the industrial bastions of the Middle West.

Any survey as brief as this has many omissions. I have said nothing of such giants as Caterpillar Tractor at Peoria, of the huge printing plants of Chicago, of the manufacturers—very large—of television and radio sets and other electronic products, of the makers of household appliances, and of the public utilities that supply the vast amounts of power that industry devours. And I have not carried through the role that the transportation facilities of the Middle West have played in the growth of its economy. Merely to list these facilities is to emphasize their importance: one of the great railroad and highway networks of the country, pipelines bringing in natural gas from the fields of the Southwest, high-voltage lines transmitting electric power generated at the minehead to distant industrial centers, the Ohio and Mississippi rivers, the deep waterway connecting Chicago with the Illinois River and the Mississippi, and finally, the St. Lawrence Seaway, giving the United States a fourth seacoast.

I dropped the story of agriculture in the Middle West at the time (1870 or thereabouts) when the farmer had survived his early hardships, if he was hardy, industrious, and lucky, and had become prosperous and even wealthy. But Robert Cass, of Sangamon County, Illinois, counting himself fortunate in the possession of 1000 acres and a snug farmhouse, could not have foreseen what would take place on his land before the twentieth century had advanced too far. He could not have known that plant geneticists—notably Henry A. Wallace of Des Moines, Iowa, Lester Pfister of El Paso, Illinois, and James R. Holbert of Bloomington in the same state—would develop a hybrid seed corn that would double yields after 1930. In all probability, Robert Cass never heard of the soybean, a leguminous plant that had been cultivated for 5000 years in the Orient, where it has been used for sauce, meal, vegetable oil, curds or cake for human consumption and animal feed, and a multitude of other products. When it was found, in the 1930s, that soybean oil could be used in the manufacture of glycerin, plastics, paints, soaps, linoleum, and other substances, cultivation spread to the United States. Since the soybean thrives in the same soil and climate as corn, the Middle West, particularly Illinois, soon took the lead in production.

At the same time that crop yields increased, two inventions speeded up harvesting and enabled fewer farmers to work larger farms. The first was the combine, the machine that makes harvesting and threshing a single process. Although a practical combine was patented in the 1870s it was not until the early 1930s, when the small combine was perfected, that the machine came to be used extensively in the Middle West. It has contributed greatly to agricultural efficiency and to the farm implement business, but at a cost in picturesqueness: stacked sheaves of wheat no longer dot the landscape in July and August, and the threshers' dinner has passed into history.

The second invention was the corn picker. As long as corn, America's great contribution to the world food supply, had been cultivated, the stalks were cut and stacked into shocks, there to stand until the late fall or early winter. About the time that the combine came into general use the mechanical corn picker, a device that had tantalized inventive minds for many years, was perfected, to be followed by the picker-sheller. Again: increased efficiency, a boon to the implement companies—and the disappearance of long rows of corn shocks that added beauty to the countryside on Indian summer days.

> At the beginning of this article I warned that I would be writing with pride and affection. Having finished, I can analyze those attitudes better than I could at the outset. Pride, I think, comes from being a small part, if only by the accident of residence, of the strongest economic

pillar of the nation. The sources of affection are more complex. First of all, the Middle West has afforded me an adequate living in a congenial occupation that, given my accent and regional provincialism, I do not think I could have achieved in any other part of the country. In the second place, the Middle West, with its informality, unpretentiousness, and lack of class distinctions, has given me an opportunity to know thousands of people of all kinds: "important" people and "ordinary" people; black people and yellow people; Greeks, Italians, Poles, and Germans; intellectuals and taxi-drivers—and sometimes the two are not too far apart. With few exceptions I have found them kind, friendly, and considerate—I am aware that the same comment might be made of the people of other sections of the country, but I know only the Middle West.

Finally the spell of the Middle Western countryside has a grip on me from which I shall never escape. I have seen many of the world's scenic beauties. I have seen the Sangre de Cristo mountains in New Mexico turn blood red in the waning light of the afternoon sun. I have seen the surf of the Pacific break in foam along the marvelous stretch of coastline between Los Angeles and San Francisco. I have seen the Mediterranean from the Amalfi Drive, and the Adriatic islands from the coast of Yugoslavia. I have seen the majestic symmetry of Fujiyama, and Orizaba framed in the bougainvillea of Fortín de las Flores. But none of these sights has blotted from mind the quiet pine forests of northern Michigan and Wisconsin, or the long vistas one sees from Terrapin Ridge approaching Galena, or the riotous colors that the wooded hills of southern Indiana take on in early October. And as I look back I think I have never seen anything as beautiful as the view from an old farmstead in Logan County, Illinois, where, from a mound only a few feet above the surrounding prairie, I looked out over miles of corn, green-gold in the late August sunshine, the epitome of Middle Western fertility, and an incomparable example of the region's quiet beauty.

God Damn Stephen Brush!
A short story

From the time I began to write professionally I wondered
whether I was capable of fiction. I thought not. I was
accustomed to dealing with facts, and I doubted that I had
the imagination that fiction required. Then one summer,
shortly after coming to Chicago, I had an experience that
seemed to lend itself to a short story.

This is what happened, and since the principal character
in the story is long since dead, I see no harm in revealing
his name. Between 1926 and 1934 a young historian
named E. Douglas Branch published four excellent books.
Two were outstanding: *Westward* (1930) and *The
Sentimental Years* (1934). Then the output stopped. Word
spread that Branch, brilliant but unstable, was having
difficulty holding teaching positions and that he was fast
becoming an alcoholic.

Shortly after World War II, Branch appeared in Chicago
and the events related in this story took place. The next
summer he came back again in much worse condition than
a year earlier. Again friends gave him as much money as
they could, but with his insatiable appetite for gin it was
not enough. Within a couple months he was arrested for
check forging, tried and convicted. A kindly judge gave
him either probation or a light sentence—I forget
which—but in a short time Branch died. I have never
known a more tragic waste of high talent.

When this story was accepted for publication the

conventional editor of *Chicago* changed my title, "God Damn Stephen Brush!" to "The Dependent." Here I have restored the original, which seems to me to fit the story better.

Mr. Brush to see you, sir," came the voice of the receptionist. "Shall I send him up?"

"Yes," said the librarian.

"The stairs or the elevator?"

"Stairs," he answered. He didn't want to make it too easy.

While the librarian waited for his visitor, he recalled what he had heard a few days earlier. In the barber shop he had sat next to Merkle, the editor of the National Encyclopedia, and they had talked as the barbers worked.

"Has Brush been in to see you yet?" Merkle had asked.

"No."

"Well, he'll be dropping in one of these days. And you'd better be ready for him, because he'll want to make a touch."

"What's happened to him? I thought he had a job in some college out west."

"Only a temporary appointment," Merkle said, "And they won't rehire him. You know he's always been a screwball, and for the last three or four years he's been drinking like a fish. I gave him some work last summer at space rates, but I had a hell of a time with him. Usually he'd show up a week after the deadline, on the verge of the d.t.'s, with a wild tale about ptomaine poisoning or something of the kind. But just when I'd have my mind made up to fire him, he'd be in on time, with his stuff done perfectly. And you know there's nobody who can write better than he can. Even encyclopedia articles."

"What makes you think he'll be back this summer?" the librarian asked.

"He always strikes for Chicago. He knows he can do a few newspaper reviews, and he thinks I'll give him some stuff. And God knows why I should, but I'll probably be fool enough to do it" . . . "Well," Merkle concluded, slipping on his coat, "See you soon."

From *Chicago*, February 1956, pp. 49–52

With Merkle gone, and the barber blessedly silent, the librarian thought about Brush. It was *The Emotional Era,* published a dozen years earlier, that had first made him aware of Stephen Brush. The book was original—a segment of American social history in which the author's full scholarship was set off delightfully by wit, irony and the grace of his writing. He had looked up Brush's earlier books—three of them. None was quite up to *The Emotional Era,* but all were good, and each was better than its predecessor. Together, they were an impressive performance for a man who at that time had barely turned thirty.

Shortly afterward, he had noticed a review signed "Stephen Brush" in one of the scholarly quarterlies. Against plodding prose and the patronizing implications of reviewers that Professor So-and-So had done about as well as could have been expected but that of course they could have done infinitely better if they had had a mind to, Brush's review flashed like sunlight breaking through gray clouds. His phrases sparkled, his comments were sound and perceptive. On an impulse, the librarian wrote him a note of felicitation. Brush replied with just the right degree of appreciation, and expressed the hope that they would have an opportunity to meet before long.

They did. A year or so later they were both attending one of the annual meetings that scholars seem to consider an essential part of their calling. Somehow Brush learned that the librarian was there, telephoned him in his room and asked whether he might come up.

The librarian remembered that meeting. The man was unimpressive—short, slender, carelessly dressed in cheap, poorly chosen clothes. Eyes abnormally large and protuberant were set in a flushed face. Long black hair was combed straight back and plastered down without a part. As far as one could tell from his appearance, he might have been a soda jerk, except that the soda jerk would have been better dressed. Only his voice gave any indication that he might be a man of unusual capacities. That was deep, beautifully resonant and marked by a tremolo that was explained in the slight twitching of his hands.

Brush talked well. His words were carefully but not obviously chosen, his sentences as perfectly formed as if he were writing them. The two men spoke of books, of mutual friends, of the futility of gatherings such as that which they were attending. But neither was at ease. Nothing struck the spark that lights a friendship. After half an hour, Brush left. The librarian had not seen him since.

But he had heard of him from time to time. Brush had left the university where he had been teaching for several years. Fired, rumor had it, after some kind of ruckus with the president. He was married and quickly divorced. Once he wrote the librarian for a letter of recommendation to a department head whom they both knew. The letter was sent and acknowledged with rather fulsome praise of the applicant, but someone else was appointed. The librarian saw occasional reviews, and it was from one of these that he learned that Brush had been on the faculty of the western college.

He heard Brush come into the outer office, but instead of going to meet him, he went through the formal rigamarole, allowing his secretary to announce that Mr. Brush was waiting, and then asking her to show him in. He greeted his visitor cordially, seated him and began a friendly but desultory conversation. Brush confirmed what Merkle had already told him—that his appointment at Missoula had been temporary, and that he was looking for another place.

"You know," he said, "I think I did rather well there, and I'm sure they would have been glad to have me stay if Maxon weren't returning from the army. At any rate, the president gave me a good letter of recommendation."

He reached into his pocket, brought out an envelope, and produced a letter already somewhat wrinkled and soiled. Before the librarian had read more than two sentences, he knew it for what it was. He had written the same letter himself; he had read it a dozen times. Smooth, commendatory, it was planned to deceive only the man whom it concerned. On the surface it said that Mr. Brush's work had been eminently satisfactory and that they saw him go with deep regret; to the initiated it read: "On the whole, we're glad to be rid of this fellow; take him on at your own risk."

"A nice letter," he commented. "You shouldn't have too much trouble landing something pretty good this fall."

"Oh, I'll have to hunt around a bit I suppose. I'll have some competition from the little boys who've learned just how Professor Big Head likes to have his behind kissed, but enough of these fellows are still in the army to give an outsider a chance. I'll connect, all right."

"What are you going to do in the meantime?" the librarian asked.

"What I did last summer—get a job at Johnston's as a night counterman and do some writing during the day. Merkle will have something for me and Jackson at the *Post* says that he can give me a review every two or three weeks."

While Brush talked, the librarian studied him. Merkle was right, he said to himself—the man's a wreck. Brush's clothes looked as if he had slept in them, his shirt, frayed at cuffs and collar, must have been at least three days on his back. The tremolo in his voice had become almost a quaver and his hands shook. Worst of all was his vividly scarlet face. The day was only warm, but sweat was soaking the fringes of his hair and dripping from his chin. Either he had a terrific hangover, or he was under almost unsupportable nervous pressure. Maybe both.

"That sounds like a pretty tough prospect," the librarian commented. "I shouldn't fancy a job behind one of Johnston's counters."

"On the contrary, I had the time of my life there last summer." Maybe it was only bravado, but he made it sound as if he meant it. "Bums, drunks, whores, cops, taxi-drivers—a gorgeous mixture. I learned more about my fellow human beings in three months than in all the other years of my life. I can't say that the knowledge was exactly ennobling, but it was a damned sight more exciting than what you find in the books. And on the whole, I'll take Mr. Johnston's patrons any day in preference to a lot of the eunuchs that infest college campuses."

By this time the sweat was oozing faster, dripping from

wrists as well as chin. The librarian took pity, and decided not to wait longer.

"It will be a little time before you have any money coming in," he said casually. "Could I tide you over?"

Although he tried to make his reply equally off-hand, Brush could not keep his voice from shaking.

"Well, yes," he said. "If you don't mind, that would be easier than getting an advance from Merkle. His place is so tied up with red tape that I was a little reluctant to propose it." The man's relief was naked.

"What will you need? Just name it."

"Will twenty be all right?"

"Of course, and more if you wish."

"I'll get paid in a few days, and twenty will see me through nicely. Thanks a lot, old man."

To show that a loan hadn't been the object of his visit, Brush talked for five minutes more before he left.

"Queer friends you've got," said the librarian's secretary after he had gone.

"He is a queer one," he replied, and then gave her a short account of Stephen Brush.

"The man's a genius," he concluded. "I knew he'd be in to make a touch, and I decided I'd let him have up to fifty dollars. I know he'll spend most of it for liquor, and I know I'll never see it again, but I don't give a damn. When a man writes four good books, the world certainly owes him fifty bucks and no questions asked. As it was, he was satisfied with twenty."

"You need a conservator," she said. But there was admiration in her eyes.

A few days later he ran across Merkle.

"Brush was in," he announced.

"Of course. How much did he want?"

"Twenty. And I gave it to him."

"You're a damn fool. You'll never see it again."

"I know it, and I don't care. See here, Merkle,"—his voice took on intensity—"that fellow has written four good books. If I could do anything as good as *The Emotional Era* I'd be prouder than those peacocks in the Lincoln Park zoo.

I made up my mind the other day that I'd let him have up to fifty dollars. That isn't going to break me, and at least he can get drunk a few times on good whisky. That's small recognition of the kind of talent he's got."

"All right, have it your own way," Merkle replied, "But I still say you're a damn fool. In three days, Brush will be that much closer to hell, and you're out twenty dollars. Who's ahead?"

"No one. You're right, of course, but I feel better for having let him have it."

Brush made his second visit a week later. This time the librarian saw to it that he waited twenty minutes in the outer office. Merkle had been right again—he was several days closer to hell. He was wearing the same suit, now more bedraggled than ever, and his linen was dirtier than before. Sweat poured from his skin faster than he could mop it up with a soiled and crumpled handkerchief. His hands shook so that the librarian had to hold a match for his cigarette. Anyone could see that he had been drunk most of the time since their last meeting.

The librarian made his visitor carry the conversation.

"I thought you might like to see some work I'm doing for Merkle," Brush said with what was intended to be nonchalance, "And perhaps you can help me with these." He handed over several galley proofs.

"Fast work," his host commented. "You've only been here a few days."

"Oh, these aren't mine," Brush explained. "These are articles as they stand now. I've got to revise them and bring them up to date. I thought you might suggest a few things I wouldn't be familiar with. The library at Missoula wasn't worth a damn, and I know that I've slipped up on work that has been published in the last year or two."

The librarian scanned the proofs while Brush mopped his face. He named two or three books, and an article in a recent issue of a scholarly journal.

"That's enough," said Brush. "If I'm not careful I'll be doing research, and this stuff isn't worth it. You know the definition of research, don't you? Use one book and you plagiarize; use two and you paraphrase; use three and that's research!" He laughed. The librarian was reminded of a boy trying, by talk, to avert punishment which he knows is coming.

"How's the counter job?" He changed the subject.

"There I had a tough break," Brush answered. "I went to Johnston's after I saw you. Sure, they'd be glad to have me again. But since last summer they've instituted medical examinations. The minute the doctor saw this"—holding out a trembling hand—"he refused to pass me. I tried to tell him that I have the tremors only when I'm nervous, as I was then, but it was no use."

"What now?"

"I don't know, but something will turn up." Brush's tone was as airy as he could make it, but his hands were shaking violently.

The librarian had intended to make him ask for it this time, but he relented.

"You'll need some more money, won't you?" he asked.

"Just enough for a few days—I'll get something from Merkle next week. I don't want to impose on you . . ."

"Quite all right. Will twenty do?"

Brush pocketed the bill, thanked him and left at once. There was no use in pretending that he had come for any other purpose.

"How much this time?" said the librarian's secretary.

"Another twenty."

"You're crazy."

He smiled.

Ten days passed before the next visit. This time, when Brush was announced, he went to the outer office to meet him.

"I'm sorry, Brush," he said coldly, "But I'm terribly busy this morning. What is it, money?"

"Yes."

Except for a word of thanks, nothing more was said. Both men knew that this was the last loan.

Weeks afterward the librarian happened to be in Poland's book shop late one afternoon. There would be no more customers that day, so Poland produced a bottle of Scotch. The talk ran to western Americana.

"Do you happen to know Stephen Brush?" asked Ed Raymond, one of Poland's best customers who was staying for a drink. "I picked up his book on the western mapmakers a few days ago. It's good."

"He's here in Chicago right now," Poland offered. "I understand he's just about gone to hell. Drinking himself to death. I don't know what the trouble is. He wrote a string of excellent books and then hit the skids. I've been afraid all summer that he'd come in and want some money. He may be in yet."

"He took me," the librarian volunteered. "Well, no, that isn't quite the way to put it. When I heard that he was in town I was sure that he would be around, so I made up my mind I'd let him have up to fifty dollars. I said to myself that I had wasted fifty dollars a good many times, and that once more wouldn't matter. And anybody who has written four good books can have fifty dollars of my money anytime—once, anyhow. Well, it took him three visits to get the fifty. Sure, I knew that he'd spend it for whisky, and that I'd never get it back. I didn't care then, and I don't care now. That's a small tribute to pay to genius." He spoke quietly, evenly, but with feeling.

"I guess you're right," said Poland. "Maybe I'd have done the same thing, maybe I wouldn't have. I'm glad he didn't put me to the test."

Rita Poland poured another drink, and the conversation drifted to other subjects.

One morning, the following October the librarian's secretary handed him a letter marked "Personal." The envelope bore the return address of a small college in Tennessee. He opened it, idly wondering who could be writing to him from there. Inside he found a blank sheet of paper and a check for 50 dollars, signed by Stephen Brush.

For long seconds he sat motionless staring at the check. Then he whispered:

"God damn Stephen Brush."

Rough Stuff I
Massacre

Before I went to live in Springfield, Illinois, in 1925, I had read many newspaper accounts and magazine articles about the Herrin Massacre of 1922. In 1925 Springfield throbbed with newer subjects: the Klan wars of 1924–26, and the Birger–Shelton gang wars of 1926–28. The stories, as I heard them from state officials, militia officers, and newspapermen, fascinated me. The fascination increased when I talked to members of the faculty of Southern Illinois University at Carbondale. I determined to write the story of violence in southern Illinois if I ever had the opportunity.

The opportunity was long in coming. I had other commitments to meet. Then I moved from Springfield to Chicago to take on new responsibilities, some of which were as foreign to me as Sanskrit. Besides, there were two men in southern Illinois who, in my opinion, were better qualified to write the book I had in mind than I was. Not until they disavowed any intention to undertake the job did I begin work. The result, *Bloody Williamson* (1952), was a sharp break with all my earlier writing. I saw the book as a challenge. Here was a brutal, inhuman explosion: could I put the brutality, the inhumanity of the participants into words that would shock readers as much as they would have been shocked as witnesses? I do not know whether I succeeded, but I do know that the book has run through several editions and is still in print. I consider it the best book I ever wrote.

The most brutal and horrifying crime that has ever stained the garments of organized labor.—*St. Louis Globe-Democrat, June 24, 1922.*

All through the night the mine guards and workmen huddled beneath empty coal-cars. Soon after sundown they were jolted by a series of explosions, and no one needed to tell them that their water plant had been blown to bits. Behind piles of railroad ties they were safe enough, even though now and then bullets spattered against the steel sides of the cars or thudded into the tough wood. But they were trapped, and they knew it.

At dawn John E. Shoemaker, assistant superintendent, and Robert Officer, timekeeper, ran from the barricade to the office to telephone for help. The line was dead. While the two men worked with the phone, shots crashed through the flimsy siding. Looking out, they saw armed men lying behind the crests of the high piles of dirt that surrounded the strip mine in which they were besieged. The men underneath the cars, now near panic, begged C. K. McDowell, the superintendent, to surrender. He agreed, reluctantly.

Bernard Jones, a mine guard, tied a cook's apron to a broomstick and came out from the barricade.

"I want to talk to your leader," he called to the men lying behind the hills of raw earth.

One of the attackers rose to his feet. "What do you want?" he asked.

Jones replied that the men inside would surrender if they could come out of the mine unmolested.

"Come on out and we'll get you out of the county," was the answer.

Behind the barricade the guards and workmen threw down their arms. As they emerged they put up their hands and formed a line. Then they walked along the railroad track and through the cut in the piles of overburden through which the spur entered the mine.

The besiegers—some five hundred miners on strike and

From *Bloody Williamson: A Chapter in American Lawlessness,* by Paul M. Angle, published by Alfred A. Knopf, Inc., pp. 3–10. Copyright 1952 by Paul M. Angle their sympathizers—surged forward, a rifle or revolver in almost every hand. They searched the prisoners and lined them up two abreast. One of the captives near the end of the line went back to the bunk car and returned with his grip. A striker took it from him.

"You won't need that where you are going," he said.

The procession started along the railroad toward Herrin, five miles to the northwest. After a short distance the prisoners were ordered to lower their hands and take off their hats. The mob grew ugly. Some of its members fired their guns into the air, some swore at the captives, and some called out to newcomers: "We got the scabs! We got the scabs!" A Negro armed with a long rifle ran up and down the line in a frenzy. Several white men urged him to use his fists on the prisoners. One of them called out:

"See these white sons-of-bitches that we don't think as much of as we do of you, colored boy!"

At Crenshaw Crossing, a hamlet half a mile from the mine, a number of men waited for the procession. The column halted. A dark, burly man with a revolver—not the leader who had promised safe conduct—waved his hat for quiet and started to talk. As the noise subsided his words carried to the frightened captives:

"The only way to free the county of strikebreakers is to kill them all off and stop the breed."

Someone in the crowd demurred. "Listen, buddy, don't rush things," he warned. "Don't go too fast. We have them out of the mine now. Let it go at that."

"Hell! You don't know nothing," the first speaker answered with a burst of temper. "You've only been here a day or so. I've been here for years. I've lost my sleep four or five nights watching those scab sons-of-bitches and I'm going to see them taken care of."

The mob, moving again, became uglier. Some of its members struck the prisoners with pistol butts, and blood began to streak sweaty faces caked with the dust raised by shuffling feet. As the crowd approached Moake Crossing, a half mile beyond Crenshaw, McDowell was bleeding from several head wounds. A cork leg made it impossible for him to keep the pace the captors had set.

"We ought to hang that old peglegged son-of-a-bitch," someone muttered.

Several times the superintendent faltered and almost fell; each time his captors jabbed him with rifle barrels and jerked him to his feet.

At Moake Crossing he stopped. "I can't walk any farther," he groaned.

The burly man who had talked about stopping the breed stepped up. "You bastard," he snarled, "I'm going to kill you and use you for bait to catch the other scabs."

He took one of McDowell's arms and motioned to another man in the mob to take the other. When the crowd moved on the three men started down a crossroad. Before the prisoners had covered a hundred yards they heard shots from the direction in which McDowell had been taken.

"There goes your God-damned superintendent," one of the mob members boasted. "That's what we're going to do to you fellows, too."

A farmer living near by also heard the shots. After a safe interval he walked down the crossroad. There lay McDowell, two bullet holes in his chest. He was dead.

At the powerhouse,* a mile farther on, the procession came to a halt.

"We'll take four scabs down the road, kill them, and come back and get four more and kill them," the leader of the column announced.

At that moment an automobile came up, and a man with an air of authority stepped out. Several of the prisoners heard him referred to as "Hugh Willis," and "the president."

"Listen, don't you go killing these fellows on a public highway," the frightened captives heard him say. "There are too many women and children around to do that. Take them over in the woods and give it to them. Kill all you can."

With that, he drove away.

---

*Where current was generated for the Coal Belt Electric Railroad, which then connected Herrin, Marion, and Carterville.

Across the tracks and to the north of the powerhouse was a strip of woodland, green with the fresh foliage of early summer, lush with the undergrowth of many years. Into it the mob herded its captives. In less than three hundred feet they came to a stout fence strung with four strands of barbed wire. A big, bearded man in overalls and a slouch hat called out:

"Here's where you run the gantlet. Now, damn you, let's see how fast you can run between here and Chicago, you damned gutter-bums!"

He fired. An instant later the woods rang with rifle and pistol shots. Several of the terrified strikebreakers fell. Those who escaped the first volley leaped for the fence, vaulting it or tearing their way through the barbs.

Sherman Holman, a mine guard, went down in the first fusillade. As he dropped, he fell across the arm of the assistant superintendent, Shoemaker, who was wounded and unconscious. One of the mob came up and kicked Shoemaker's body.

"The son-of-a-bitch is still breathing," he said. "Anybody got a shell?"

A man with a revolver stooped over and sent a bullet into the assistant superintendent's brain.

William Cairns, another guard, was part way through the fence before his clothing caught. While he struggled to free himself he was shot twice. He fell, but he could still see and hear what went on around him. Not far away a strikebreaker, spattered with blood, leaned against a tree, screaming. With every scream someone hit him. One of the mob lost patience.

"You big son-of-a-bitch, we can kill you," he said. Then he drew his pistol, and fired.

The strikebreaker crumpled to the ground.

Edward Rose, also a guard, wriggled through the fence, but not far beyond it tripped and fell. With the attackers close behind his only chance was to lie still and hope that he would be taken for dead. The bearded man who had fired the first shot noticed him.

"By God! Some of 'em are breathing," he announced.

"They're hell to kill ain't they?"

He fired, hitting Rose in the back. The wounded man remained conscious. From the ground he could see boots swing as their wearers kicked men who had been shot, and he could hear pistols crack when bodies gave signs of life. The shooting moved into the distance, but now and then a faint scream gave notice that some terrified fugitive had been trapped. Finally the noise died away.

Miraculously, some of the strikebreakers emerged from the barbed-wire fence with only cuts and scratches. Most of them simply deferred their fate.

Between the powerhouse woods and Herrin lay a strip of timber known, from its owner, as the Harrison woods. About 8:30 in the morning Harrison and his son, working in the barn lot, heard shooting to the southeast. As they turned in that direction they saw a man running toward them, with fifteen or twenty others in pursuit. Several of the pursuers stopped and fired. The fugitive fell. The Harrisons watched three or four men drag the body into the timber. A few minutes later another group came up with two prisoners at gunpoint. They too disappeared in the trees. Shots followed. After a safe interval father and son walked to the spot where the men had entered the woods. There they found a body hanging from a small tree. Three other bodies lay beneath the dead man's feet.

One of those who vaulted the fence at the powerhouse was Patrick O'Rourke, a mine guard from Chicago. In the woods he was hit twice, but since he was still conscious and able to move, he hid in the underbrush and his pursuers missed him. When they had gone he started up a road toward Herrin. On a bend a car caught him by surprise. He ran to a near-by farmhouse and hid in the cellar, but the occupants of the automobile had seen him. All were armed, and he had no choice but to surrender when they ordered him out of his hiding-place. As he emerged, one of the men hit him over the head with a pistol butt, and then they dragged him to their car.

By this time other cars had stopped and a small crowd had gathered. Some wanted to shoot the captive, others to hang him. During the argument a newcomer reported that five more prisoners were being held at the schoolhouse in Herrin. O'Rourke's captors decided to take him there.

In the schoolyard the prisoners—now, with O'Rourke, six in number—were forced to take off their shoes. Someone in the mob made one of the captives, a World War veteran, remove his army shirt. Then all were ordered to crawl on their hands and knees. After fifty or sixty feet they were allowed to walk again, though still without their shoes.

The crowd, some two hundred in number, headed for the Herrin cemetery, a mile distant. They were in a vicious mood, kicking and beating the bleeding prisoners as they stumbled along the road. Even the children—and there were many in the mob—yelled "scab" and other epithets at the captives.

At the cemetery, the procession halted. As the prisoners stood on the highway bordering the burial ground, several members of the mob came up with a rope and yoked the six men together. Once more they were ordered to move on, but they had covered only a short distance when word spread that the sheriff was coming. Taunts came from the crowd:

"God damn you, if you've never prayed before you'd better do it now!" and in derision: "Nearer my God to Thee!"

Two or three shots were fired. O'Rourke, hit again, fell to the ground, pulling the other five with him. More pistols cracked, and the stricken men writhed in agony. After their bodies were quiet one member of the mob filled the magazine of his revolver and methodically fired into each inert form.

In a few minutes three of the men on the ground showed signs of life. Thereupon one of the bystanders drew a heavy pocketknife, knelt, and slashed the throats of those who still lived.

About 9:30 Don Ewing, a Chicago newspaperman, arrived at the cemetery. O'Rourke and a man named Hoffman, both partly conscious, were calling for water. Ewing found a small pail, filled it at a near-by house, and started to give Hoffman a drink.

"Keep away, God damn you!" a bystander warned, and

backed the threat with a cocked rifle.

A young woman holding a baby taunted the dying man: "I'll see you in hell before you get any water." As she spoke, she casually put her foot, and part of her weight, on the man's body. Blood bubbled from his wounds.

Without protest from the crowd, one of the mob urinated in the faces of the victims.

About midmorning, when it was perfectly safe to do so, Sheriff Melvin Thaxton of Williamson County, and one deputy, took up the trail of the mob. Wherever they found dead and wounded men they called for ambulances and undertakers. Those still alive were taken to the Herrin Hospital; the dead were sent to a vacant storeroom in the same city. There they were stripped, washed, laid on pine boxes, and covered with sheets. Then the doors were opened, and for hours men and women (often with babies in their arms) filed past. Some spat on the corpses; some said to the children whose hands they held: "Look at the dirty bums who tried to take the bread out of your mouths!"

Late June in southern Illinois is hot, and the door of the improvised morgue had no screen. Long before nightfall flies blackened the wounds that still seeped in the eighteen bodies.*

*Another body was found the following day.

Rough Stuff II
The Hanging of Charlie Birger

Joe Adams, the mayor of West City, a town on the border of Benton, Illinois, was an ally of the Shelton Gang, mortal enemies of Charlie Birger and his gangsters. In December 1926, two young men appeared at Adams's front door and killed him. Birger was charged with murder—the indictment was a rare one, accessory before the fact—and convicted on July 27, 1927. Various appeals delayed the imposition of the death sentence until April 19, 1928.

For many years I had qualms about having quoted Birger's remark, "It *is* a beautiful world," attributed to him just before he was hanged. It seemed too pat, too likely to have been the invention of some newspaper correspondent. Three or four years ago I expressed my doubts to my old friend Milburn P. Akers, in 1928 head of the Associated Press bureau in Springfield, Illinois. "Forget it," he said. "I was there, and I heard him say it."

All through the night of April 18, while thousands crowded into Benton in the hope that they might see the execution, Birger talked—to his jailers, to newspapermen, to his lawyer, to the rabbi whom he had refused to see until these last hours of his life. He talked of everything that came into his mind—of his boyhood; of his years in the army; of his first wife who, he said, was the best of the four he had

had, though he didn't have sense enough to know it when he was married to her; of the crimes he had committed and of those he was charged with. He prayed with the rabbi, and told him he wanted to do what was "right toward God" for the sake of his sister and children.

"Good-bye, Bob, old boy," he said to Smith when the lawyer finally left his cell. "I know you have done all you can, and I thank you from the bottom of my heart."

To the last he denied that he had plotted the murder for which he was to die. Yet he spoke with no resentment. "They've accused me of a lot of things I was never guilty of, but I was guilty of a lot of things of which they never accused me, so I guess we're about even."*

At seven o'clock on the morning of the 19th he ate a hearty breakfast. When a doctor offered him a hypodermic he refused it.† The barber entered his cell to shave him, but the man's hand shook so badly that he could not continue. Birger took the razor and carefully went over his face himself. Then he dressed in a gray suit, tan shirt, and dark striped tie.

At nine-thirty, surrounded by guards, he left his cell. As he passed other guards in the corridor he called out in a voice that carried no hint of nervousness: "Good-bye, boys, be good!" When he stepped into the jail yard and saw the mounted machine-guns he remarked: "Looks like the western front here."

Smiling, he walked briskly to the scaffold and mounted the steps. He looked at the crowd in the enclosure and at the other hundreds at windows and on rooftops outside the stockade. The spring sun came out from behind a cloud, and he turned his head to the sky.

---

*Reliable evidence indicates that Birger was suffering from general paresis. There is no reason to believe, however, that the malady had progressed to the stage of mental or moral irresponsibility.

†One of Birger's lawyers writes me: "He didn't need a shot. I have always understood that he was hopped up to the limit. I suspect that he had dope at any and all times during his imprisonment. He always was able to win the complete acquiescence of some of the jailers to permit him to do whatever he wished, including sleeping occasionally with his wife."

"It *is* a beautiful world," he said.

Looking down again he waved to an acquaintance. Then he spoke to the faces before him in a quiet, even voice.

"I have nothing against anybody. I have forgiven everybody, all because of this wonderful Jewish rabbi. I have nothing to say. Let her go."

Those near the scaffold saw that he was still smiling when the black hood came down over his face. The hangman fastened the noose, and the sheriff sprang the trap.

In a few minutes life left the body of the man who had sworn that he would kill Joe Adams and that there was nothing "the God-damned Franklin County law" could do about it.

To The Memory of Benjamin Platt Thomas: 1902–1956

How does one write a memorial to a very close friend? I faced that problem after Ben Thomas's death, when I was asked to assess the meaning of his life for the *Journal of the Illinois State Historical Society.* I could describe his contributions, which were of the utmost importance, to Lincoln literature, but if I limited myself to that phase of his life I would only be turning out the impersonal kind of sketch that one expects to find in the *Dictionary of American Biography.* On the other hand, familiarity in biographical writing has always offended me. So I hit upon two approaches: the formal, in which I recorded the public career of Benjamin P. Thomas as objectively as I could; and then after a clean break, a highly personal sketch of the Ben Thomas whom I had known and loved.

My daughter, a professional editor whose judgment I regard very highly, happened to be at home when I pulled the last sheet of this manuscript from the typewriter. "Read this," I asked. "Pop," she said twenty minutes later, "you made me cry."

Death seems to be most tragic when it gives no warning. The suddenness of the announcement that came on the

From the *Journal* of the Illinois State Historical Society, Vol. L, No. 1 (Spring 1957), pp. 6–23 evening of November 29, 1956, that Benjamin P. Thomas had died that afternoon, gave a special intensity to the sorrow of his friends, while the fact that he was in the full vigor of middle age made his loss seem needless to the many thousands who knew him only through his writings.

Benjamin Platt Thomas died at the age of fifty-four. He was born on February 22, 1902, at Pemberton, New Jersey, the only child of Benjamin Platt and Martha Johnson Thomas. His father died when the boy was two years old. After two years of widowhood his mother married Ernest Ward Pickering, a silk worker who soon gave up his occupation to enter the Baptist ministry. The stepfather took his wife's son as his own and provided a happy home for the boy, modest but comfortable.

After attending high school in Baltimore, where the family then lived, young Thomas entered Johns Hopkins University. There, majoring in economics, he made a scholastic record that won him election to the Phi Beta Kappa Society in his senior year. But he was no grind. In addition to being a convivial member of the Delta Upsilon fraternity he was a first-rate second baseman, captain of the Johns Hopkins team in his last college year and a proficient semi-pro, under an assumed name, on Sundays. (Perhaps it should be explained, for the benefit of the uninitiated, that a college baseball player loses his amateur standing when he plays for money. In Thomas' case, the time-honored practice of using an assumed name was made the more advisable by his ministerial father's objection to Sunday baseball.)

After graduating in 1924, Thomas taught for a year at St. Paul's Choir School, a small private school for boys in Baltimore. He liked teaching, but the ascetic conduct required of instructors irked him. In the summer of 1925 he decided to put his academic training to use and went to work for a Baltimore investment house. Selling bonds was not especially difficult in the booming Twenties, but Thomas soon realized that he had not found his life work. In the fall of 1926 he returned to Johns Hopkins as a graduate student. He had had enough of economics. For the next three years he would devote himself to history. Under the influence of John H. Latané, head of the department and an authority on American diplomacy, Thomas chose Russian-American relations as his special field. His dissertation, entitled "Russo-American Relations, 1815–1867," was duly accepted, and at the end of the academic year 1928–1929 he was awarded the degree of Doctor of Philosophy.

The dissertation, published in 1930 by the Johns Hopkins University Press, caused no great stir, but a number of highly respected journals found space for notices. Two reviewers, one in the *American Historical Review* and another in *The Journal of Modern History,* complained that the author had used no Russian-language sources—he had not, in fact, learned the language—but such equally authoritative publications as *The International Journal of Ethics* and the *Revue Internationale de Sociologie* praised the book as clear, scholarly, interesting, and a useful contribution to the subject.

By the time *Russo-American Relations* appeared, two important events had happened in Thomas' life. He had been appointed associate professor of history in Birmingham-Southern College at Birmingham, Alabama, and he had married (December 26, 1929) Salome Kreider, of Springfield, Illinois, whom he had met while she was a student at Goucher College.

Thomas stayed at Birmingham-Southern for three years. He liked college teaching even better than he had liked teaching at preparatory school, and he soon became one of the most popular members of the faculty. He knew his subject thoroughly, he lectured fluently and with wit, and he had an easy approachability which, with his youth, appealed strongly to the student body. The college saw him leave in 1932 with real regret, tried to lure him back two or three years later, and in 1955 took pride in conferring on him the degree of Doctor of Literature.

On his part, Thomas had no dissatisfaction with Birmingham-Southern. He simply saw a more inviting opportunity in Springfield, Illinois. In 1932 the secretaryship of the Abraham Lincoln Association became vacant. Logan Hay, the Association's president, had a summer home at Old Mission, Michigan, where the Kreider family also spent their vacations, and through meetings there had come to have a high regard for the young professor's ability. Hay offered Thomas the position. The Association was a small organization which had functioned effectively for only seven years, but it offered more time for historical research and writing than an associate professorship. The change, moreover, attracted Mrs. Thomas. Thomas accepted, and took up his new duties in the fall of the year.

The new secretary's first piece of writing appeared in the December, 1932, issue of he *Bulletin* of the Abraham Lincoln Association: an article entitled "Old New Salem." A. L. Bowen, the discerning editor of the *Illinois State Journal,* paid a graceful and merited compliment: "Mr. Thomas is master of a most pleasing literary style and he has dressed an old subject in attractive new garments. In a long time I have not read a better written or more interesting bit of history."

The duties of the Association's executive officer were varied. He supplied information on Lincoln's life to all who requested it, served as a guide to writers and distinguished visitors, did what he could to obtain new members, and arranged for the annual meeting and dinner. But his principal responsibility was research and writing. In his initial article Thomas had pointed to the first subject he would undertake: the full story of New Salem and the restoration of the village that was then in progress.

In writing this book, as he admitted many times later, he learned the historian's craft. To produce even a paper under the close scrutiny of Logan Hay was something of an ordeal, but one learned more than any graduate faculty was likely to teach him. Thomas himself put it well when he wrote, in *Portrait for Posterity:*

Although Mr. Hay always insisted that the various Association secretaries should have full credit for the books that bore their names as author, a great deal of him went into everything they wrote. Constantly peering over their shoulders as they worked were his kindly but questioning eyes. As a critic he was unexcelled; with loose writing or loose thinking he was merciless. When one made a statement or offered a conjecture in his presence, he had better be prepared to back it up.

Every sentence in *Lincoln's New Salem* was weighed and analyzed. Passage after passage was rewritten until it met Logan Hay's approval. In the process a competent piece of writing became a brilliant one.

The book was small and its publisher, the Abraham Lincoln Association, obscure. General recognition was not to be expected. Yet one of the country's most distinguished critics picked *Lincoln's New Salem* for a full-column review in the *New York Evening Post*. Describing it as a "fascinating piece of Lincolniana," Herschel Brickell called its publication an event no less important than the reconstruction of New Salem itself. "A contribution to the Lincoln saga of the first order," he concluded. The book would go through four editions and is still in demand.

As soon as Thomas finished *Lincoln's New Salem,* he plunged into a second book: a continuation of the "Day-by-Day" series which had been started with the publication of *Lincoln: 1854–1861* in 1933. His assignment was the period, 1847–1853. One can hardly imagine a more disagreeable job of research. Thomas did not exaggerate when he wrote:

> It involved an enormous amount of tedious, dirty work in newspaper collections, court files, legislative and congressional records, and a multiplicity of miscellaneous sources; but it did not lack thrills and satisfactions. The present writer . . . well remembers the days he spent in dingy courthouses, usually in the basement, turning the interminable pages of dusty ledgers, poring through grimy files long undisturbed. Invariably the clerks declared it was a waste of time—no Lincoln documents had been found for years. Yet, in every single instance documents were found, and in one courthouse they numbered a hundred or more.

The book that resulted from such labor as this—*Lincoln: 1847–1853*—was a reference tool, and though a valuable one, its publication went practically unnoticed. To this day the book has not received the attention it merited, for of the four volumes in the series, this alone had an outstanding introduction. The reader who wants the best account of these eight years in Lincoln's life, when the future president realized his long-standing ambition to serve in Congress only to see his political career fade out in failure, will find it here. Liberal excerpts from this introduction, reprinted in *The Lincoln Reader,* led Lloyd Lewis to characterize Thomas as "an independent researcher of Springfield whose discernment and originality of approach have long entitled him to greater recognition in the field."

By 1936, when *Lincoln: 1847–1853* was published, Thomas had served four years as secretary of the Abraham Lincoln Association. Beyond question he had succeeded, yet he was not entirely satisfied. Routine work cut deeply into time for research, and personal responsibilities were making increasing demands. Mrs. Thomas' family had substantial property interests with which Thomas found himself becoming more and more deeply involved. He was discovering, moreover, that he had an aptitude for business, and that he liked it. After long reflection, he decided to resign his position.

With Carlos W. Campbell, Thomas formed the general insurance and property management firm of Thomas & Campbell. The partners soon found that Springfield offered an insufficient opportunity for property management, but they prospered in the insurance business. Before long the original firm consolidated with an existing agency to become Weller & Campbell, and thrives today under that name.

Thomas soon entered another occupation. In a property division, Mrs. Thomas came into possession of a sizable farm twenty miles east of Springfield; her husband undertook to manage it. He knew nothing of farming but he learned fast, studying agricultural bulletins and periodicals, even taking short courses at the College of Agriculture of the University of Illinois. He poured fertilizer into the depleted soil, improved yields, and bought purebred Polled Herefords. Cattle shows came to be a regular feature of his life. In an amazingly short time he transformed a run-down farm into a productive and profitable one. This achievement, along with his personal affability, led to an honor which he valued highly: election as president of the Illinois Polled Hereford Association.

For eight years Thomas devoted himself to business and farming. His firm prospered, the farm prospered, and he became such an integral part of Springfield's business community that the Chamber of Commerce elected him its president. Yet history never released him. He maintained his memberships in the Mississippi Valley and American historical associations, and the less-than-lively professional journals held a high place in his extensive reading. In 1944 he decided that more than anything else in life he wanted to write history. He disposed of his interest in the insurance business and set to work.

His decision was a courageous one. He could not know that he would succeed—his published output was too small to be an indication. He knew that he would raise some eyebrows, for Springfield would never quite understand why a man who could make money in an orthodox occupation would turn to something of such doubtful legitimacy as writing. And he would be lonely. The writer's calling is a solitary one, and oppressively so when unrelieved by association with those who accept his usefulness without question.

Thomas first thought of expanding his Russo-American study into a full-sized book. The end of World War II was near, and no one needed to be a prophet to be sure that Russia would play a large part in the world of the future. He soon realized, however, that he had been out of the field too long, and that the library facilities of Springfield could not begin to supply his needs. But for almost any phase of Lincoln's life the Illinois State Historical Library offered unsurpassed resources. The life of Lincoln had been his specialty. Why leave it?

A subject soon engrossed him—the biographers of Lincoln. How different they had been—the proper Holland, bent on making Lincoln an orthodox Christian; wild Billy Herndon, bent on making Lincoln an infidel; Nicolay and Hay, pledging their word to Robert Lincoln that they would strike from their work any part of it which he disapproved. Thomas would describe the methods and points of view of these men and their successors, and in the process, he hoped, do something to clarify the portrait to which all had contributed.

Nearly three years went into the writing of the book—three years which took the author from the Henry E. Huntington Library to the Library of Congress and to a dozen institutions in between. In the early fall of 1947 *Portrait for Posterity: Backstage with the Lincoln Biographers* was published by the Rutgers University Press, then headed by Thomas' good friend, Earl Schenck Miers. The critical reception was immediate and enthusiastic. *Time* and the *New Yorker,* highly selective media, gave the book favorable reviews; long notices appeared in the *New York Times,* the *New York Herald Tribune,* the *Saturday Review.* Thomas was particularly pleased by a review in the *Charleston* (South Carolina) *News,* in which the reviewer, after confessing that he had always looked on Lincoln as "considerably less than a God," admitted that the War President emerged "more human and appealing than many biographers had made him."

Portrait for Posterity was a critical success, but its sale, while respectable, was not large. Thomas was disappointed though not discouraged. At the urging of Earl Miers he began to collect material for a book on the Abolitionists. Before he had progressed far he found that Theodore Dwight Weld, a half-forgotten leader of the anti-slavery movement, was usurping the story. Abandoning his original plan, Thomas turned the book into a biography of Weld which Rutgers published in the fall of 1950. Again the critical reception left nothing to be desired. The popular book review sections, "class" magazines like the *Survey Graphic* and the *New England Quarterly,* and the professional historical journals all found the Weld biography a highly commendable achievement. Again there was one review that gave the author a special chuckle: a favorable notice in the *Southwestern Historical Quarterly* signed Jefferson Davis Bragg!

But *Theodore Weld, Crusader for Freedom* stayed on bookstore counters. Commercially, the book was a failure. This time Thomas was discouraged. It is all very well to tell an author that he should find his compensation in the satisfaction that comes from a task well done, but such consolation is rarely offered by those who have devoted three years of their lives and a considerable amount of money to the writing of a book that fewer than two thousand libraries and individuals are willing to buy. Better advice is that which several of Thomas' friends, and particularly Earl Miers, pressed upon him: Don't give up; keep writing and sooner or later you will come up with a book that will sweep the country. He decided to stick it out.

Thomas learned a lesson from the Weld biography. Weld was a minor character, and few people cared about him. To write a great book, one must have a great subject. What greater subject could one have than Abraham Lincoln? The time was ripe for a biography that would synthesize the results of a quarter-century of research and still stay within the limits of one volume. Miers, now on the staff of Alfred Knopf, tendered a contract, and Thomas plunged into the subject.

In little more than two years *Abraham Lincoln, A Biography* was in bookstore windows. (The time-span is deceptive: knowledge acquired over many years cut research and writing to a fraction of what they would have been otherwise.) To give even the merest sampling of the enthusiastic reviews is likely to tax a reader's patience. *Time* proclaimed: "To Benjamin P. Thomas, a college-professor-turned-Illinois-cattleman . . . goes the distinction of writing the best one-volume life of Lincoln since Lord Charnwood's version of 1916." Lewis Gannett (*New York Herald Tribune*) wrote that "henceforth, when the question is asked, 'What is the best single volume that tells the whole story of Abraham Lincoln?' the answer is likely to be, 'Thomas'.'" Sterling North (*New York World Telegram*) appraised the book as "a keen, perceptive, reliable, complete one-volume biography of Lincoln which should be in every home and school in America." Allan Nevins (*Saturday Review*) found it "much the best single-volume life of Lincoln yet written." "A truly excellent piece of work," said Bruce Catton (*Cleveland News*) ". . . a permanent addition to our Lincoln literature—one of the

finest additions that have been made in many a year." Gerald
W. Johnson (*New Republic*) noted particularly its excellent
English style, "plain and simple, but balanced and rhythmic
that often rises into eloquence but never drops into bathos."
Max Eastman (*The Freeman*) labeled it "the most exciting
book" he had read in the whole publishing season.

This time the buyers responded. *Abraham Lincoln* made
its way into the best-seller lists, climbed in rank, and held
its place for many weeks. Foreign editions began to appear,
and kept coming out until there were ten in all: British,
German, French, Spanish (for Mexico), Slovenian, Greek,
Arabic, Korean, Japanese, and Chinese (for Formosa). To
Knopf went an Honorable Mention under the 1952 Carey-
Thomas Award for Distinguished Publishing.

In a variety of ways, *Abraham Lincoln* brought recognition
to its author. Lincoln College, Knox College, and Northwestern University conferred honorary degrees. (Illinois College
had anticipated them in 1947; Birmingham–Southern would
follow in 1955.) He was invited to join, and did join, the
Phi Beta Kappa Associates. The *New York Times,* the *New
York Herald Tribune,* and the *Chicago Tribune* asked him
to do book reviews. He was in demand as a speaker; his
graceful performances in this difficult role brought him more
invitations than he could accept. In short, he achieved almost
instant acceptance as a full-fledged, full-time, successful
writer.

Thomas had considered, after finishing the *Lincoln,* a life
of Stephen A. Douglas, but had turned instead to a biography
of Edwin M. Stanton, Lincoln's Secretary of War. This he
interrupted, however, to edit the Civil War reminiscences
of Sylvanus Cadwallader. Cadwallader had reported the war
for the *Chicago Times* and later, for the *New York Herald.*
Late in life he wrote a long account of his experiences which,
after some years, came into the possession of the Illinois
State Historical Library. There it languished, little used, until
Earl Miers gave it a thorough reading and urged Thomas
to edit it for publication. Knopf agreed. Thomas performed
the usual editorial functions of cutting out repetitive passages, correcting errors, and supplying an introduction. In

1955 the book came out under the title, *Three Years With Grant.*

Within a few weeks, the editor found himself the object of a rough, relentless attack. The Cadwallader memoirs had attracted him by what he considered to be the author's "clear view of how the Civil War was fought at the command level," by Cadwallader's vignettes and appraisals of leading Union officers, his intimate picture of Grant. Thomas had not been unmindful of the sensational character of a passage describing Grant on a prolonged drinking spree, but he had accepted it as only more conclusive evidence of the Federal commander's already well established propensity occasionally to overindulge.

This was the passage, included in an excerpt from *Three Years With Grant* published in *American Heritage* for October, 1955, that touched off the controversy. The first letter came from U. S. Grant III, protesting strongly the publication of a story that he described as "fantastically untrue and scurrilous," and criticizing the editor of *American Heritage* for not having put it aside for investigation "before defaming unjustly one of our country's great men." (Thomas, familiar with the bibulous habits of the Fathers of the Republic, could not see why the story of Grant's binge constituted defamation.) The second and very much longer letter came from Kenneth P. Williams, author of *Lincoln Finds a General.* Here the attack was directed as much at Thomas as at Cadwallader. Williams not only questioned the editor's competence; he also charged him with deliberate distortion. Thomas was hurt deeply. He had admired Williams' work, and he could not understand why Williams' criticisms should be so personal and so bitter. Thomas' reply, published with the two letters of his critics in the August, 1956, issue of *American Heritage,* revealed his wounded feelings. The subject still preyed on his mind at the time of his death.

Controversy, no holds barred, was not a role which came easily to Benjamin P. Thomas. When he felt compelled to make an adverse judgment in reviewing another writer's book, he did it gently. He knew how difficult it was for the biographer or historian to avoid error or misinterpretation, and he would be charitable rather than harsh. This was both his nature and his reasoned conviction. Speaking to the girls of Ferry Hall on the occasion of his daughter's graduation in 1953, he said: "The mark of an educated person is a certain humility born of the realization of how little he possesses of the sum total of human knowledge. There is nothing quite so tragic or so dangerous as the ignorant complacency of the man who knows it all." And writing, in *This I Believe*, of any fellow human being, he asserted quietly: "I do not blame his offenses on his race or his creed or his color, remembering that I, and men of my race, creed and color also fall short and offend."

It is not farfetched to assume that Thomas' basic convictions were derived, at least in part, from his long study of Lincoln's life. Certainly he believed as firmly as Lincoln in democracy, not only as a form of government but also as a social system in which all men had equal rights. "You, more than any other generation," he told the students of Ferry Hall, "will be called upon, again and again, to ask yourselves the simple but all-important question, 'Do I believe in democracy or don't I?' And if you answer 'Yes,' as I sincerely hope you will, then you must help to make the ideals of democracy something more than platitudes to be mouthed on suitable occasions." Those ideals were more than platitudes to him. He hated—literally hated—Senator McCarthy for his tactics and for the cleavage he rived in what had generally been a tolerant and unified people. He was deeply disturbed by the failure of many Southern communities to follow the Supreme Court's desegregation decision, and seriously considered canceling an important trip to New Orleans not long before his death because of his revulsion at what he took to be human retrogression.

In the summer of 1956 Thomas began to suspect that he had cancer of the throat, but he did not seek an examination until the end of November. His physician confirmed his suspicions. Three days later, unwilling to subject his family to anxiety and anguish that could have only one end, he took his life. On December 1, after funeral services at the First Presbyterian Church, which he had recently joined, he was buried in Oak Ridge Cemetery.

Here, perhaps, this account should end. But I must add a few paragraphs. Ben Thomas was my close friend for twenty-five years; Sally Thomas, his widow, is my friend; and I have watched George, Martha, and Sarah Thomas grow from infancy to maturity. If I were to record only the fairly obvious facts of Ben Thomas' life I would be false to the obligations of both biography and friendship.

In what I have written, Ben Thomas appears without the smile or chuckle that was never far beneath the surface. In life he was witty, humorous, even funny. One of his most appealing qualities was the gift of mimicry. He had an uncanny ear not only for peculiarities of English speech but also for dialect. I remember, on one occasion in Chicago, sending him to the barber whom I have patronized for years, partly because Joe is an excellent barber and partly because, after thirty years in this country, he speaks the most amusing blend of English, Italian, and American profanity that I have ever heard. Ben returned in half an hour and, as I had hoped he would, reproduced Joe's conversation to the last mixed syllable.

Ben could do, and often would under a little stimulus, a monologue in pseudo-Russian that would bring tears of laughter to any audience. The dialect itself was amusing enough, but the real attraction of the performance was the wise, witty, and ever-changing commentary that he clothed in comic language. I do not exaggerate when I say that I have heard nothing like it since the days of Will Rogers. The monologue, always spontaneous, sometimes produced an epigram or a hit that surprised even Ben himself. When that happened he would burst into laughter, and the performance would stop until the performer recovered his composure.

He loved to sing, especially the old evangelical hymns and the popular music of that idyllic period that came to an end with the first World War. One of the most vivid memories of a long friendship is a night at the "Gay Nineties" in New York. There the entertainment was—and I suppose still is—songs of fifty and sixty years ago with the audience joining in. At "A Bicycle Built for Two" Ben's eyes would take on a soulful look, his heavy shoulders would sway with the music, and every now and then he would break out with what he called the "soft shoe"—a perfect vocal imitation of the sound of soft shoe dancing. Many times, around pianos in the homes of friends, I have seen him enjoy himself in the same way, all the while giving more pleasure than he suspected to others in the group.

He was adept at pantomime. He could impersonate to perfection the batter facing a pitcher who could smoke a ball in so fast that it would thud into the catcher's glove before the batter could take the stick from his shoulder. The routine included all the orthodox practices of the batter—knocking the dirt from cleats, hitching up pants, stepping out of the box a split second before the pitcher delivers—as well as facial expressions denoting amazement at the pitcher's speed and disgust at the umpire's ball-and-strike calls. I have seen Ben do it innumerable times, and it has never failed to transport me from someone's living room to a ball park.

The performance was symptomatic of Ben's interest in sports. Baseball was his first love. In the years when Springfield had a team in the Three-Eye League, Ben and Sally were often in the stands. When the spring meeting of the Mississippi Valley Historical Association was held in a city with a big-league ball team, Ben and I usually managed to skip one session and take in a game, just as we often succeeded in working in a burlesque show in those cities where that now-outmoded form of entertainment had survived. For years Ben followed high school football and basketball even to the point of accompanying the team out of town. In the last weeks of his life he had a running bet with a friend on the television boxing matches they both watched on Friday nights. The day before he died he wrote a note: "If 'Black Pants' wins tomorrow night, pay Al a dollar."

Ben liked cards, and recognized the fact that a little money on the outcome of a game gave zest to it. For years, with our wives, we played bridge every week or two. Ben played a game to my liking, meaning that every now and then he would ignore the conventions to make a wild bid that would either pay off in a high score or cost a heavy penalty.

For years, too, he was one of a group of friends who played rummy—not fancy gin rummy but the good old saloon variety of the game—at each other's homes once or twice a month. Here the stakes were higher, but we were all evenly matched, and even with a run of bad luck no one suffered more than a few days' dearth of pocket money.

I must not give the impression that Ben spent an inordinate amount of time in such frivolities as those which I have mentioned. For every hour that he and I leaned over a card table I should guess that we spent at least two hours in more or less serious talk. (Given fluency, he would not mind my admitting, by a highball or a glass or two of beer.) Very often, but by no means always, our subject was history—its significance, its techniques, its practitioners. I shall never forget Ben's travail during the months Logan Hay subjected the manuscript of *Lincoln's New Salem* to his incomparable criticism.

After an evening's session, when we walked away together, Ben would explode: "Damn it, Paul, I can't be that bad!" But the next day he would manfully meet Mr. Hay's objections. In the end he would admit—more than that, he would volunteer—that the book was far better than it would have been without those sessions that so severely taxed his patience.

Ben was particularly grateful for Logan Hay's tutelage because he believed that through it he learned a great deal about historical writing. On that skill he put a high premium. In his opinion, history was worthless if it was not readable. In his own writing he developed the faculty of self-criticism, revising repeatedly for clarity and movement, especially movement. He had difficulty with clichés—who doesn't?— and, like all formally trained historians, he had to guard against a tendency to academic ponderosity, but he knew his faults and generally overcame them before a manuscript reached final form. Stylistically, he was at his best when his subject permitted a glint of humor or touch of satire.

Ben liked the companionship of historians and writers. He attended most of the meetings of the principal historical societies—not because he would learn anything from the formal sessions, but because for a few days he could associate with men whose values were the same as his. He was especially fond of a group from Illinois College whose members had dubbed themselves the "One-Two-Three Club." (The reader will have to guess the meaning of the name.) When, in Chicago, the Civil War Round Table and the Caxton Club met on successive days, Ben could be counted on to be present. He spoke several times before both organizations and had many friends among their members.

He had friends everywhere. Everyone liked him—businessmen, cattlemen, historians, writers, publishers. He made no effort to impress or to be ingratiating; he was simply himself—kindly, gentle, humorous, interesting. It was a happy coincidence that on the afternoon we lowered his body into the grave the grass should still be green, the sun warm and golden. The day fitted his nature as the tomb of Lincoln, not far away, stood for his life achievement.